Alterity

STUDIES IN VIOLENCE, MIMESIS, AND CULTURE

Alterity

Jean-Michel Oughourlian
Translated by Andrew J. McKenna

Michigan State University Press · *East Lansing*

Original French Edition
L'Altérité
©2020 by Groupe Elidia Éditions, Desclée de Brouwer
10 Rue Mercoeur 75011 Paris / 9 Espace Méditerranée 66000 Perpignan

Michigan State University Press
East Lansing, Michigan 48823-5245

Library of Congress Cataloging-in-Publication Data is available
ISBN 978-1-61186-451-9 (Paperback)
ISBN 978-1-60917-726-3 (PDF)
ISBN 978-1-62895-494-4 (ePub)
ISBN 978-1-62896-488-2 (Kindle)

Cover design by David Drummond, Salamander Design, www.salamanderhill.com.
Cover art: *Narcissus* (ca.1597–99), oil on canvas, by Michelangelo Merisi da Caravaggio (1571–1610)

Visit Michigan State University Press at *www.msupress.org*

We possess within ourselves a reserve of ready-made formulae, designations, expressions, which are pure imitations that free us from the task of thinking and that we tend to take for valid and appropriate solutions. . . . This is why it is difficult for us to take ourselves at our word. I mean that the words that come to mind are, generally speaking, not our own.

—Paul Valéry, Variété III, 1936

Contents

Preface

A somewhat mild attention to ourselves teaches us that a
book is the product of another self than the one that we
manifest in our habits, in society, in our vices.
　　　—Marcel Proust

What is a "good life, a "successful life"? To this question Luc Ferry
(2002) has devoted admirable pages, outlining the history of
human thought from Greek antiquity to the modern age; he writes
about the different conceptions of the way that humans need to inscribe themselves into the natural, social, and religious world, in order to attain happiness.

For the Greeks, the good life consists in finding one's place in the universe, the cosmos. Once this topos, this abode, is found, they needed to
dwell in it in such a way as to participate in the harmony of the universe. The
good life for the Greeks refers us to a transcendent alterity. It is the same in
revealed religions: the good life is one that conforms to the commandment
and prescriptions of God. Divine transcendence, absolute otherness, is the
unique point of reference for the three revealed religions.

In our disenchanted world, which has been "liberated" from all transcendence, a successful life is evaluated in terms of total immanence, in

each person's self-realization. We are "to take responsibility" for who we are, develop "self-confidence." Personal fulfillment has become the goal. As Julia Funès writes in *Développement (im)personnel*, "henceforth nothing counts more than personal flourishing to justify one's existence," adding "the sole valid criterion of a successful life has become the self." But on the basis of my work with René Girard since 1978, and more recently in *The Puppet of Desire* in 1982, I maintain that the self does not exist on its own. So all the therapies that consist in reinforcing it are spinning their wheels.

In this new book, I pursue my research, aiming to demonstrate the unity of living beings, and to show that the toxic mechanisms and pathologies operating in physical illnesses and in psychological disorders are similar. Their cause? Alterity.

There is alterity from without, such as infectious diseases, and alterity from within, such as cancers. In psychopathology, alterity fluctuates, sometimes in the form of a model and friend, at other times in the form of a rival and enemy. Just as healthy cells in the stages of cancer are transformed in order to hide their aggression behind the mask of certain enzymes, so too with mental problems, where an enemy otherness hides behind symptoms in order to camouflage an unthinkable or unacceptable rivalry; they find expression instead in a distress of some mysterious origin.

For physical illnesses, as for mental disorders, the cure resides therefore in the recognition of the rival alterity, in a lucid gaze at reality; in both cases, we must not be mistaken about the adversary. In the following pages, I shall elaborate on these problems and propose some principles of intelligibility that can help to avoid the misrecognized pathogen.

Vertical Alterity

The myth of creation poses the question of alterity at the outset. By breathing upon the world God (the personage thus named in biblical mythology, Creator of the earth and the sky, then of humans), begets a human being, the first man, Adam, who is suffused with alterity. Everything comes to him from the Other. Next, according to the exegetes, comes Eve, who God created from a rib of Adam, and so issuing from a double alterity, coming from God and from Adam.

On the psychological level, the entire history of humanity raises the question of alterity. The human being is born from the union of two gametes; his mother gives him life and brings him into the world. He cannot deny the alterity of his biological as well as his cultural origin, since, from his earliest moments, the human will be steeped in the culture of his parents, beginning with his "mother tongue."

From this point on, in biblical tradition, human beings engender one another mutually. The reproduction of humans from generation to generation, which goes back to God's creation of the first man and the first woman, exhibits the vertical alterity of every human being.

The creation story of Adam, then of Eve, in the text of Genesis has aroused myriad philosophical and theological debates, notably with respect to Darwin and the scientific reality of the evolution of species. I, for my part, have always considered the texts of the Old Testament as myths that nonetheless raise the most fundamental issues for us as humans. In several books, I have argued that the myth of an earthly paradise and of the "fall" from it, labeled as "original sin," is an extraordinary psychological lesson. I have held that the psychology of Adam and Eve is mimetic, and that the character of the serpent is an allegory of rivalrous mimetic desire at the origin of every "fall" "since the foundation of the world."

God separates; he creates woman by separating her from man, by otherizing a part of Adam. The serpent divides by injecting in Eve the venom of mimetic rivalry; the serpent disconnects humans from the divine: humans can no longer live in paradise, in the garden of Eden, and are thrust into the world as we know it, the one infected by mimetic rivalry, which is the fountainhead of all conflicts and every form of violence. This world is "governed" by a venom, a poison that is mimetic, and this explains why, in certain Judeo-Christian texts, the devil is called the Prince of this world.

II.

Horizontal Alterity

I n *The Puppet of Desire*, I explain at length how the "self" is a product of desire. It is in vain that the "self" asserts ownership of "its" desire; it is the offspring of desire. I propose a new metapsychology, one founded of the "self" of desire, each desire producing a different "self." I show the relevance of this by analyzing the phenomenon of hypnosis in the course of which the desire of the hypnotizer is substituted for that of the hypnotized subject. This person's "self" disappears; it is replaced by a new "self," the other "self" of the other desire or of other's desire, and this new "self" bears new features: a new consciousness, a new memory, a new voice sometimes, or even a new age, as when the mesmerist suggests that the subject is five or ten years old. We have learned from René Girard that desire is mimetic, and therefore, mapped on to another's desire; it is generated, incited, by the desire of the other. Generally speaking, the "self" is constantly produced and refashioned by a horizontal alterity that shapes it at every moment. Nonetheless, the "self" does not see it that way. All our psychologies and psychopathologies illustrate the strategies and tactics of the "self" to assert ownership of "its" desire, of desire as such, in order to affirm his anteriority with regard to another's desire, which nonetheless induces, suggests, produces it.

	Model	Rival	Obstacle
Normal Structure The other is real and recognized but forgotten.	Recognition of difference: Learning, identification, hypnosis	Vengeance Envy Jealousy	Renunciation or substitution of desire
Neurotic Structure The other is real and misrecognized.	Pathomimia Possession Adorcism Mythomania	Diabolic possession and exorcism Hysteria	Resentment Psychasthenia Obsessions and compulsions
Psychotic Structure The virtual other is designated, accused, suspected, or hallucinated.	Paraphrenia	Paranoia Chronic hallucinatory psychosis	Schizophrenia (fragmentation, dispersal)

For further clarification, in *The Mimetic Brain*, I review different schema according to how the other is perceived and experienced as a model, a rival, or an obstacle. I illustrate here by reproducing above the complex table that I had developed. It will allow us to account for the way the metamorphoses of the model into rival or obstacle radically modifies the clinical schema and how the diagnosis can shift from one category to another. This is why psychopathology must never lose sight of the flexibility and mobility of symptoms and syndromes.

Avatars and Problems Posed by Alterity

A few years ago, I dined with René Girard in Paris. I had just spent some months delving into the study of Hindu sages: Jiddu Krishnamurti, Maharishi, Ramesh Balsekar, Sri Aurobindo, Ramana Maharishi, and others, including the singular personage of Gurdjieff.

Goaded by my readings in transcendental meditation, I raised a question weighing on my mind: "If you meditate deeply and sound yourself out, what will you see?" Girard answered without hesitation, "You will see your mediator." He used the word "mediator," which is to say the model, to signal the mimetic relationship between the model and the disciple, and to underline the begetting of the disciple's desire and its modeling on the desire of the mediator as that which draws the subject to the object that the model signals as desirable. His answer stimulated further and firmer reflection.

Of course, my first thought was that the ultimate revelation that occurs to us during the deepest meditation is that of alterity. In the depths of ourselves, the Other is the double alterity, vertical and horizontal, that constitutes us, as I mentioned earlier.

The revelation of alterity poses several problems, whose solutions can give rise to all sorts of controversies—philosophical, ethical, religious, political, and, as I see it, psychological and psychopathological as well. Alterity raises the question of freedom and, therefore, of responsibility. It raises the question of equality, which obsesses the French in particular. It raises the problem of my "self," of my person, of my originality, my singularity, my identity. I have explained at length in my books what is at stake for psychology and psychopathology: the "self" asserts ownership of "its" desire in commonplace, banal circumstances as well as in stages of neurosis and psychosis. Desire in turn claims its priority, its anteriority to the desire of the model it copies. Here again, this assertion can take place in normal, peaceful circumstances, where we talk about "identification"; or in neurotic or psychotic conditions, as we saw in the table earlier.

————————————

Before continuing, and looking back over centuries and theories, I wish to emphasize that I find the revelation of alterity has known two striking, really fundamental moments: vertical alterity, with the creation of man and woman by God; horizontal alterity, with René Girard's discovery that desire is mimetic, mapped onto the desire of a model.

It is the desire of another that gives rise to, that creates, the "self." "My" desire generates a "self" that corresponds to it. As I explain in *The Puppet of Desire*, this is why the "self" is an unstable entity, in constant metamorphosis, suffused with alterity. The whole history of psychology and psychiatry reflects the efforts of Culture, conceived as the system of scientific knowledge and beliefs of any period or civilization, to circumvent, explain away, or contain this alterity. There are assorted strategies, be they commonplace, neurotic, or psychotic, that each and every one across centuries has fashioned within a particular cultural and anthropological backdrop, in order to assert ownership of "my" desire and my anteriority to any other's desire.

Psychopathology begins when the model turns into a rival or obstacle and the "sick person" refuses to recognize it as such; instead, we disguise it, hide it behind various masks, physical or mental. This deep-seated process, which is an active negation of reality, the refusal to acknowledge and confront rivalry, is what I have identified as "misrecognition," "méconnaissance" in French, in order to highlight, with Girard, its active nature. It is probably this hidden reality that Freud labeled the unconscious, which he saw as the cause of an illness and of its pathological symptoms; whereas the term misrecognition highlights the active process that aims at the negation of reality: the refusal to see the model as the origin of "my" desire, this other's desire that produces my "self," and the transformation of the model into a rival or an obstacle. It is therefore the active negation of alterity, henceforth toxic, that causes the symptoms and the illness, and not some obscure and complex unconscious montage, whose invention aims at restoring ownership of its desires to the "subject," to the "self," while at the same time removing responsibility for its effects.

To elucidate what I have just said, I will relate the case of Emily as illustrative. I met her husband, Bernard, at a conference, where he told me: "My wife, Emily, suffers from an illness that the doctors and psychiatrists cannot seem to cure."

"What is she suffering from?"

"She makes involuntary gestures abruptly, impulsively. For example, her arm strikes out, knocking over a glass, or inadvertently hitting the face of the person across from her. Sometimes her leg gives way, and she falls painfully."

I gave Bernard my business card, and he came to see me occasionally to talk about his wife, who refused to see a new doctor. He told me he was a writer and so could work from home and not leave his wife alone, for they adored each other. She would read his work in progress and offer useful suggestions.

The couple appeared perfectly happy, but . . . one day, Bernard confessed that he was sexually frustrated. At my inquiry about that, he confided that he desired his wife, whom he found beautiful and desirable, but she, while sleeping naked with him in the same bed, would reject any caresses, any intercourse whatsoever. She might let him stroke her breasts but refuse to go further. He was trying to cope with his frustration.

One day, he told me that his wife's symptoms worsened. She would smash objects and that depressed her. She was disheartened and cried a lot. I told him that that "depression," which she acknowledged and which upset her, called for intervention. He proposed going to a clinic to treat her malaise. She agreed, and I came on board as a "specialist" of this illness.

After a few days at the clinic, a mild antidepressant and some tranquilizers produced rapid improvement. In the course of numerous sessions, she sang the praises of her husband and told me how much she loved him, how she could not live without him. He, for his part, told me he could accept sexual frustration in order to keep her and protect her. That surprised me coming from this forty-year-old strapping fellow. Not understanding, I wondered about Love . . .

Years pass and Bernard comes frequently to see me. We become friends, sometimes have a drink together. I have appointments with his wife, whose symptoms fluctuate, so I adapt her dosage. She is better, then less well, but she tells me she trusts me. One day, Bernard divulges a curious arrangement. His wife has a friend, her "best friend," Catherine, who is a lawyer specializing in literary property. She becomes Bernard's lawyer and soon Emily invites her to move in with them and she does. They live in a large house in the suburbs because Emily loves to garden and be with her beloved dogs.

A few months later, Bernard tells me he has rented an apartment in Paris in order to write and work closely with his editors. He goes there twice a week, and Catherine spends two days with him there to assist him. Emily, he tells me, takes this very well; she does not wish to leave her home.

Somewhat later, Bernard invites me over for a drink and introduces me to Catherine. He was keen on my meeting her because they have a problem: they have become lovers. Bernard tells me that he recaptured his zest for life with the revival of normal sexuality. But this is their big problem: do they tell Emily about this or hide it from her? Bernard does not wish to hurt his wife, whom he loves, and Catherine does not want to anger her best friend!

I tell them that I agree with their desire not to traumatize Emily and advise them to "give time to time," a fashionable expression of the day.

A few months pass. Emily wants an appointment. She enters my office in a state of great agitation. "I suspect," she says, "my husband and Catherine are having an affair. This is unacceptable, monstrous." She complains of an exacerbation of her aberrant symptoms and describes a distress and a fury that have replaced her depression, evidencing a maniacal state. She rages, she tells me, howling and throwing herself on the ground, shaking with convulsions. I prescribe neuroleptics to at least reduce her maniacal fury. She leaves me with a promise to keep me informed.

A few days later, Bernard phones me to say he has left home because his wife was impossible to live with. Emily phones me the next day to tell me: "Bernard has left home; I suspect he is living with Catherine. On the other hand, your new treatment helps me. I am less agitated, I sleep better, and, after giving it a lot of thought, I have contacted my lawyer to ask for a divorce!"

The divorce process goes on for months, during which I help her as best I can, and Bernard and Catherine as well, without telling Emily. One day, Emily phones me to say: "I have finally got rid of that bastard. The divorce went through." To my inquiry about her psychological state, her answer stupefies me: "I am fine. I have almost stopped with the prescriptions. I am calm. I am not falling down. I read. I garden. I play with the dogs. I am happy!"

My interpretation is that her "cure" was due to recognizing her rival, whence the disappearance of the symptoms whose role was to conceal the toxic, rival alterity. In the beginning, Bernard was her love and therefore her model. Then for miniscule reasons, impossible to pinpoint, the model had slowly transformed into the rival, perhaps owing to a certain literary jealousy on her part. The alterity became unbearable. The active misrecognition of the rival alterity had been hiding behind physical and mental symptoms of unknown "origin." Therefore the "cure" was due to recognizing the toxic alterity, to identifying her rival; it was due to her conscious awareness of the transformation of the initial model into a rival, which had involved what I call the second brain, where emotions are triggered, where love morphed into hate. Since it was unthinkable to detest her husband, she fell ill! And the cure consists in recognizing the transformation of the one's model into a rival; the cure requires the strength or the courage to face up to reality, despite inhibitions about this, despite religious, moral, social precepts, or financial interests.

Once the rival is identified as such, one can forsake or at least avoid that person. This is why I have always taught that, in the therapist's office, there are always three entities: the doctor, the patient, and the illness (neurosis or psychosis, or another illness of desire). What is at stake is whether the patient wishes to align with the therapist to get free of the engrossing rival alterity that produces all the disturbing symptoms—or whether the patient will align with the pathogenic other in order to show the inanity of the therapist and the futility of his efforts.

I open a parenthesis here to recall attention to my classification of the cerebral functions of what I call the "three brains":

- A cognitive, intellectual function that we call rational, or first brain, essentially corresponding to the neocortex and comprising motor and sensorial zones, and in the left temporal lobe the language zones.
- An affective, emotional function, located essentially in the limbic brain, which I have called our second brain, which is host to feelings, sentiments, love, and hate.
- And finally, a third brain, the mimetic brain, which is the first to come into play in our relations with another, who is apprehended straightaway as "model," "rival," or "obstacle." This third brain can be activated by mirror neurons, and I have the feeling that all neurons in this brain have a "mirror function." This brain is an enormous mimetic machine that can operate for the best or worst, as we shall see further on.

IV

A Concise History of Alterity

continue with my now virtual dialogue with René Girard, since he is no longer with us to respond. The question that I wish to raise is as follows: "Why has it taken almost five thousand years after Aristotle for imitation, mimesis, to be recognized as a fundamental mechanism that is operational in the outbreak of violence, both on the level of whole societies and in the processes of psychology and psychopathology?"

In fact, Aristotle (*Poetics* 4.1) had rightly emphasized that the little *anthropos* is the most "miming" of animals, and that it is by imitating that our species accumulated all our skills. Spinoza, much later, also accentuated the contagious character of emotions and desires. Gabriel Tarde devoted numerous studies to imitation, though without perceiving all its consequences.

At a conference that I organized in Besançon in 1995 (*Le Désir: Énergie et finalité*), René Girard presented a text by Montaigne relating the misadventure of Alexander's soldiers in India when surprised by a horde of aggressive monkeys. At once the soldiers armed themselves with their swords and lances, but Alexander ordered them to drop them, and instead to get ropes and vines and tie one another up with them. Upon seeing this, the monkeys did what their nature commanded: they imitated the soldiers, tying up one another, which enabled the soldiers to escape from them. But we had to wait until René Girard to realize that mimesis lies at the origin of violence and the sacred, activating the most universal and fundamental psychological mechanisms, where runaway reciprocal hostility focuses on a scapegoat, whose unanimous destruction results in a peace attributed to a divinity.

In an article that recently appeared in *Alternative santé* about my book, *Cet autre qui m'obsède*, Gary Laski reduced Girard's idea of mimesis to "a footnote to Hegel's *Phenomenology of Mind*." Without being a specialist on Hegel, I had already studied, with the help of Alexandre Kojève's *Introduction to a Reading of Hegel*, the difference between desire in Hegel and mimetic desire. In Hegel, desire is the desire of the other, the desire to be desired, and therefore to be admired and recognized as superior to the other. This is the dialectic of the master and the slave foreshadowing class struggle as we find it in Marx. In other words, desire in Hegel is a particular case of mimetic desire where the model is systematically taken for the rival. This is not a desire to copy the desire of another, but one that aims at being the object of the other's desire. It is a desire for recognition by the other of my superiority as to what he has or what he is, such that in violent combat I will deprive the other of the envied property or being. Since I lack these, I will satisfy myself with depriving him of them. This is what I called negative mimetic desire.

To wish to dispossess the other of what he *has* is the class struggle, communism, the fanaticism of equality. Recently, this has taken shape in the moralization of "public life" in France, which consists in depriving elected officials of their financial advantages. In *Le Figaro* of May 10, 2019, Michel Delacomptée quotes La Bruyère:

> We have for the grandees and those highly placed in our world a sterile jealousy or impotent hatred that does not recompense us for their splendor or preferment, but only adds to our own misery the unbearable weight of others' good fortune.

The malady of equality, which is effectively the mythical demand of uniformity, had already been decried by Shakespeare in *Troilus and Cressida* (1.3.75–137) in Ulysses's complaint of dissension and disorder in the ranks ("O, when degree is shaked, / Which is the ladder to all high designs, / Then enterprise is sick!"), where rivalry proliferates throughout. Girard reminds us that "degree" means "hierarchy," therefore difference, therefore acceptance of alterity. Franz-Olivier Giesbert, in *Le Point* of April 2019, points out that, according to Hippolyte Taine, social ranks in the ancien régime were clearly delineated, ambitions were "limited," such that envy was attenuated. Giesbert concludes: "After that, envy is liberated, and with it, hatred, jealousy, bitterness, malevolence, pessimism, all the 'sad passions' identified by Spinoza that proliferate in our society." For Michel Delacomptée, this resonates with Shakespeare and René Girard: "We are threatened by the reign of the undifferentiated, which produces chaos and violence. There is no harmony without alterity. I think, along with Levinas, that alterity is foundational."

To wish to surpass or dispossess the other in his or her very *being* is terrorism, Islamist or other, that of Baghdadi as well as of Robespierre. To terrorize, in fact, you have to kill, massacre, torture a part of the population; they are accused of every evil, and thereby deemed as an inferior group (*Untermenschen*); they are superfluous, toxic. The result is to deny them the status of human beings and to arrogate the right, if not the duty, to eliminate them.

Finally, one can wish to dispossess the other of the object of his or her desire or at least thwart its realization. This case brings to mind the judgment of Solomon, which I will discuss shortly, but first I wish to illustrate the second case, as brought up by the psychiatrist Chawki Azouri in one of chronicles published in *L'Orient-Le Jour* (n.d.),

> A Lebanese legend tells the story of two men condemned to death. The officer in charge asks the first one: "What is your last wish before dying?" This one answers: "I wish to embrace my mother for one last time." The officer asks the other of his last wish and he answers: "My last wish it that you should prevent the other man from embracing his mother for the last time."

To return to the judgment of Solomon (1 Kings 16–28), two women have been sleeping in the same space, each with her newborn infant, and one of them has smothered her baby while sleeping; she places it at the breast of the other sleeping woman and takes the living infant to breastfeed it. Upon awakening, the first woman finds the dead child by her side and realizes that it is not hers. The two women quarrel and bring the case before King Solomon:

The king says: This one says "this is my son, the living one, and your son the dead one." And that one says: "No! Your son is dead and mine is living." The king says: "Cut the infant in two and give one half to each mother."

The mother of the living infant overcomes her rival desire, her mimetic rivalry, and prefers to save the life of the infant, surrendering the object of her desire. This attitude allows Solomon to understand that she is the true mother and gives her the living infant.

We could multiply similar examples. The traps of mimetism and mimetic rivalry are innumerable. In these detours and dead ends, many "patients" lose their bearings, and often so does many a therapist. There is but one path leading to the pure and simple reality of psychological functioning, the path opened up by René Girard. If this reality has been avoided for such a long time, it is because it raises the fundamental problem of alterity: accept the idea that my desire is not mine, not spontaneous, not self-generated, does not belong to my "self"; that my desire is copied, is a borrowed desire—all that is very difficult and even contrary to the Hegelian desire for recognition discussed a moment ago.

But to claim ownership, and thus anteriority of desire to that of another or all others, raises a second difficulty: if I am the owner of a desire spontaneously born from within, I am responsible for it, whatever the consequences. This is at once false and unacceptable: false because, as we now know, the desire is mimetic, imitated, copied, suggested by a model's desire; and it is inacceptable, because to assume the consequences of "my" desire can lead me to an unbearable guilt, and lead others to disapproval, even punishment. I turn now to an historical overview of these two problems.

In Genesis 1:26, Elohim says: "We shall make Adam in our image." Adam, formed out of the earth, out of dust, is thus entirely suffused with alterity. In *The Puppet of Desire*, I propose we read "in our image" as the inscription by God in man of the first dimension of universal mimesis, the spatial dimension of imitation. God's desire for creation is obviously not mimetic, but that of Adam is henceforth purely mimetic. I hypothesize that what is transmitted here is the desire to create. Humans are made to create the other, to create themselves endlessly, and to create around ourselves.

But Adam can do nothing all alone; God is going to create an additional alterity, as we read in Genesis 2:18: "Elohim said: It is not good for the man to be alone; I will make a companion for him." Eve is created, according to all the translations, out of a rib from Adam, from out of his side. She too is suffused with alterity. She will be for Adam a helpmate, surely, but along side him, as an equal. But mimesis comprises not only imitation, but rivalry. In fact, from the very beginning, rivalry is consubstantial to mimetic desire as the rest of the story shows. The serpent, allegory of mimetic desire, will inject Eve with the venom of mimetic rivalry, in getting her to take God for a rival and no longer a model, a rival who wishes to deprive her of a divinity reserved to Him.

Henceforth, whatever is forbidden is desirable. This shows, too, the mimetic origin of curiosity, a positive value for scientists, a terrible flaw for certain others. In any case, curiosity is only awakened when something is hidden, inaccessible, or mysterious—whence the prohibition. I have explained this at length in *The Genesis of Desire* (chapter 2), and I only want to emphasize one aspect of it here. When God angrily accuses Adam of having disobeyed him and eaten of the forbidden fruit, Adam recognizes the alterity of his desire and at the same time declares his irresponsibility: "The woman whom you gave me gave me the fruit and I ate it" (Gen. 3:12). Asked about this in turn, Eve also invokes the mimetic prompting of her desire as an excuse: "The woman said: 'The serpent deceived me and I ate'" (Gen. 3:13).

And so from the dawn of history we find the problem of the alterity of mimetic desire along with the problem of responsibility. In many various forms, we find this throughout human history. Before proceeding, I want once again to return to this sentence in Genesis: "God created man in His image." As I see it, God imprinted in humans the first dimension of universal mimesis, imitation, but the mimetism does not necessarily concern every aspect of the model. To imitate is not to copy; imitation is not copying. What imitation does God propose to humans? I think God transmits to us what He has just accomplished: creation. The creatures can create in turn, create descendants, create the world around them, create themselves endlessly, recreate themselves in a movement of continuous self-creation, by way of recurrent, progressive initiations.

In his book *La Maladie de l'âme*, Jackie Pigeaud studies the problem of dualism and monism in antiquity. We learn that the expression "sickness of the soul" is from Plato, and Pigeaud specifies that "by monism or dualism, we are to understand nothing less than the feeling that each one has of being one or two." This "integral" duality will be debated all across the history of medicine, philosophy, and psychiatry. At the beginning of my studies, psychosomatic medicine was in vogue and the literature on this is too massive to cite it here. I myself published with my advisor and friend, Jacques-Marie Coldefy, chief surgeon of the psychiatric hospitals in Paris, a book entitled *Approche psychosomatique de la pratique médicale et chirurgicale.*

The Greek physician Galen, Pigeaud tells us, insisted on the somatic origin of madness, while maintaining an indisputable dualism. Other doctors have not been as exacting as Galen. Consequently, a dualist can admit that there are primary sicknesses of the soul that affect the body, and primary sicknesses of the body that affect the soul. This second view is decidedly modern. Everyone today knows what disorders and physical symptoms can lead to stress and anguish. What's more, we know that the first symptoms of a cancer of the pancreas, for example, can be anxiety or depression.

In one of the fragments of Democritus, we read "the doctor treats the illness of the body. Wisdom frees the soul from its passions" (cited in Pigeaud, 17). This debate still goes on today. In the entire history of medicine and philosophy, dualism conceals alterity at the same time as implying it. In fact, the soul and the body are not of the same nature. The soul in particular is a mysterious entity and its definition has spawned endless philosophical debate. Thus dualism establishes two different processes; the soul and the body are essentially different. Alterity is therefore implied by this duality but is concealed by the radical difference we make between them. Nonetheless, the solution to this aporia is to be found in the recognition of a real alterity, the two "others" being of the same nature.

Here is Jackie Pigeaud again (67): "Galen thinks that Apollo is right to require that one know oneself," but, he adds, "self-knowledge is through others" (10). In his *Treatise on the Passions*, Galen affirms: "It is to others to diagnose what we are, not to ourselves," and he specifies what will become our therapy—in our time, psychoanalysis: "We have to choose someone who neither loves nor hates us." Farther on, he emphasizes the requirement of "scrupulous, minute attention of the chosen interlocutor, because this person must point out to the patient the smallest things that precisely elude his or her consciousness." This requirement could have come from Freud.

To avoid alterity, we double down. Jackie Pigeaud summarizes (274) as follows: "Plutarch has admirably sensed this in his *Treatise on Ethical Virtue*:

'The rational soul is to the irrational soul what the soul in general is to the body.'" So we have an analogy: the irrational soul is the body of the soul. In his *Tusculan Disputations*, Cicero asserts (in Pigeaud, 246) two essential facts: "the triumph of the body/soul dualism"; the idea that between emotions, passions, vice, and madness, there is no difference in nature, only in degree.

In his *Treatise on Mental Alienation*, Philippe Pinel (in Pigeaud, 246) echoes Cicero, affirming that the origin of madness is passion, and that the passions are illnesses. So the passions are the concern of medical practice, and doctors need to become philosophers. Cicero, along with Pinel, is endowed with medical authority, and better still, therapeutic authority. Ever since Cicero, dualism has prevailed. This will be famously endorsed by Descartes. For Cicero, "the illnesses of the body need a doctor who is an outsider, but it is not the same with the soul, where, everyone must be his own doctor" (in Pigeaud, 252). In the entire subsequent history of what we call psychosomatic medicine, alterity goes around in a closed circuit between "my" body and "my" soul. What is this "self" that owns a "body" and owns a "soul" and what evidence have we for its unity given the relations between two agencies that are essentially different in nature?

Responsibility for bodily illnesses will be found, with Pasteur, to originate in bacteria and viruses. Responsibility for illnesses of the mind is the subject of debates that go back to Plato, to whom I shall return shortly. As for the reciprocal causality and the mutual influence of body and soul, this has become the abundant pièce de résistance of twentieth-century research. This research is preoccupied with stress, a psychic phenomenon, and with description of its physical and somatic consequences. At an early period, the discovery of tranquilizers, and in particular of benzodiazepines, appeared as a miracle cure; for the past thirty years, patients are progressively more apprehensive of the treatment than of the illness. This is why stress, anguish, and all the neuroses treated by psychotherapy—Eye Movement Desensitization and Reprocessing (EMDR), hypnosis, and lately meditation—are gaining ground, since they do not have the side effects of psychotropic drugs.

V

Toward the Discovery of Alterity

An eminent psychosomatician, H. P. Klotz, had proposed representing the word "psychosomatic" in a closed circle, a seamless feedback loop with no discernible point of origin, in order to illustrate the undefinable relation between soma and psyche, their continuity and mutual causality. The causality is in fact circular, and we are going around in circles. The problem of alterity and responsibility had been voided by their dualist dialectic. It is time to return to origins and revisit those who have posed the right questions, even if they have given the wrong answers.

The first fundamental text is *Timaeus*, where Plato discovers a hostile and built-in alterity:

> And the seed having life, and becoming endowed with respiration, produces in that part in which it respires a lively desire of emission, and thus creates in us the love of procreation. Wherefore also in men the organ of generation becoming rebellious and masterful, like an animal disobedient to reason, and maddened with the sting of lust, seeks to gain absolute sway. (91b)

Two problems arise here, whose evolution requires attention: the problem of desire and its origin, and the problem of alterity. The male organ demands satisfaction and is "disobedient to reasoning" as it affects the person and determines his behavior. In men, the independence of the male organ in relation to their will is obvious, but Plato continues:

> And the same is the case with the so-called womb or matrix of women; the animal within them is desirous of procreating children, and when remaining unfruitful long beyond its proper time, gets discontented and angry, and, wandering in every direction through the body, closes up the passages of the breath, and, by obstructing respiration, drives them to extremity, causing all varieties of disease. (91c)

The cause of the illnesses is therefore the frustration of an *intra-physical* other, whose agitation is the cause for both men and women. Alterity is integral to the body, but endowed with its own desire, whose satisfaction is pathogenic. The man and the woman *are acted on by the other within them*, and whose dissatisfaction has adverse consequences. Aretaeus of Cappadocia confirms this view:

> In the middle of the flanks of women lies the womb, a female viscus, closely resembling an animal; for it is moved of itself hither and thither in the flanks, also upward in a direct line to below the cartilage of the thorax, and also obliquely to the right or to the left, either to the liver or spleen; and it likewise is subject to prolapsus downwards, and, in a word, it is altogether erratic. It delights, also, in fragrant smells, and advances towards them; and it has an aversion to fetid smells, and flees from them; and, on the whole, the womb is like an animal within an animal. (2.9, "On Hysterical Suffocation")

We find the same independence of the male sexual organ, which can lead to satyriasis, a term derived from the lustful Satyrs presiding at Dionysiac revelries, which today we call priapism: "The lust for sexual intercourse is ungovernable, and is unappeased even after many continuous gratifications" (2.7, "On Satyriasis," p. 55). Thus the male sexual organ is an animal within the animal, independent and predominant. Aretaeus continues:

but I do not at all believe that [women] are affected with Satyriasis, for their nature, being cold, is not adapted to it. But neither, also, has woman the parts necessary for erection, like those of a Satyr, whence the affection derives its name; and neither also are men subject to suffocation from the womb, because men have not an uterus.

Thus for Plato, for Aretaeus, and a whole line of thinkers and doctors extending to Ambrose Paré, the sexual organ is an independent animal that imposes its desires to its bearer, and makes him or her ill if it is not satisfied. The alterity of desire is affirmed; it is due to the presence of an *intra-physical* other. Neither men nor women are responsible for desires imposed upon them. The problem of freedom is foremost. The treatments proposed for this indisposition were picturesque. The uterine animal was reputed to detest nauseating odors and to like pleasing ones. Thus Ambrose Paré advocates sniffing malodorous "salts" to subdue the "animal," and perfumes between the thighs to conduct it toward its natural place.

With Christianity, and notably the teaching of Saint Augustine, Platonic theories and those of the Greek doctors are refuted on the grounds that God could not have created an imperfect being; it is unthinkable that He should ordain a pathogenic otherness. Noticeable mental disorders are therefore assigned to an *extra-psychic* other: the devil, who can possess, obsess, tempt humans, imposing desires on them and making them ill, or insane, or otherwise miserable. The treatment of suffocation of the uterus and of satyriasis well be consigned not to doctors laden with perfumes, but to ecclesiastic judges, exorcists, inquisitors. The incubus, the succubus, and witches of all sorts are punished and burned at the stake so as to be purified of the demon's work.

In *The Puppet of Desire*, I told the story of a famous case of demonic possession in Loudon in seventeenth-century France. Mother Jeanne des Anges declared herself possessed and prey to crises that today we would call hysterical; she accused the priest Urbain Grandier of having been the instrument of the devil and having possessed her. Of course, she had never seen Grandier; she had only heard about him, a fact that proved that the devil was the responsible agent. The inquisitors and exorcists came into the scene. Demonology is manifold in this culture and the devils are named and classified hierarchically. The unfortunate priest was burned alive.

Thus Mother Jeanne is found innocent of a desire that has been imposed on her by the devil, an extra-psychic other. She is not responsible for this desire and the pathological disorders in its train. But Mother Jeanne is unhappy about not being the owner of her desire. Much later, she will write her memoirs where we find her trying to reconcile the possibility of being the owner of her desire without for all that being responsible. She concludes her memoires with this sentence, one that opens the way to a new psychological outlook: "I was acted upon, but I was acted upon by myself."

Mother Jeanne's contention reprises that of all humans throughout time. She wishes at once to be the owner of her desire and at the same time not to be responsible for its consequences. This contention explains the fierce resistance to René Girard's hypothesis from the outset. Mimetic desire in effect deprives the "subject" of ownership and anteriority of its desire, but at the same time rids it somewhat of any responsibility. The only responsibility, the only freedom of the "self" is the choice of the model. Well-being consists in the recognition of the eventual metamorphoses of the model into a rival or an obstacle.

But Mother Jeanne will get a hearing with a great twentieth-century psychiatrist, Sigmund Freud, who affirms that my desire belongs to me, that it is generated by my self, but that I am not responsible for it, because it is unconscious. Thus Freud dominates his culture and ours, granting us ownership of our desire all the while exonerating us of responsibility. Freud invents an *intra-psychic other*: the unconscious, which directs us without our knowing it. This brilliant solution will predominate in psychology and psychiatry and all the human sciences. It is the reason why Girard's theory of mimetic desire has been so difficult to accept. For he shows, in fact, that my "desire" is not original, that it does not emerge from within the "self," but rather that it is suggested by another, being mimetically mapped onto the desire of another. It is borrowed desire, and for that very reason, denied all the more frenetically. The energy and finality of desire come from the Other whose desire is the model for "my" own.

Thus, for René Girard, the alterity of desire is real, tangible; the model is divulged. I very quickly adopted this view, which appeared to coincide with reality. In part 2, chapter 2, of *Things Hidden since the Foundation of the World*, Girard and I elaborated an *interdividual* psychology, invalidating the notion of individuality, of the human monad, the subject.

I have since then pursued research in this direction. As of 1981, I proposed a new metapsychology, that of the "self" of desire; mimetic desire generates the emergence of a "self" that is quickly adopted. The "self" is a variable, unstable entity, but precisely for that reason I maintain that it forgets "its origin," or, on the contrary, lays claim to its ownership and anteriority frantically over against the relation that inspired it. Everything happens as if desire maintained its anteriority over against the relation to the model desire, the desire of another, the desire suggested by another and that this desire imitates.

This is how I was led write in *The Mimetic Brain* that Culture, despite some reticence, was disposed to accept, namely, that desire is mimetic, but that neurosis and psychosis persist in denying this, since they hold to the self's ownership of its desire and its anteriority to another's desire. Hysterical neurosis represents the other by alienating, otherizing, a region, an organ, or a bodily function, and by holding it to be autonomous, or, to recall Arataeus, "moved of itself hither and thither." But in fact this organ represents the rival as responsible for the illness or dysfunction. This is how neurosis succeeds in representing alterity and avoiding responsibility.

In psychosis, the pathogenic alterity is alienated to a part of the psyche most often in the form of hallucinations, auditory or kinesthetic. Here again, alterity is responsible for everything. It is represented, but concealed in order to allow, once again, for claims of ownership for "my" desire and its anteriority to that of another, thus rejecting mimetic desire and consigning responsibility to an extra-psychic alterity.

We could say, therefore, that mimetic desire is the unconscious agency par excellence. We have seen that Girard prefers "misrecognition" (*méconnaissance*) to "unconscious," for it acknowledges an active dimension to the process. For my part, I have maintained in *The Mimetic Brain* that recognition is the route to a cure, to genuine insight. This recognition can only take place with the help of another or others by a process that is not simply cognitive or emotional; it is a process of transformation, a kind of initiation, that has been the life and the teaching of all the great initiates.

VI.

Alterity in the Creation of Man and Woman in Plato and Greek Mythology

---

Alterity is the subject of Plato's *Symposium*. Phaedrus declares: "Since it is the most ancient, Eros is for us the source of the greatest goods" (178c); he goes on to say: "I conclude for my part that Eros is the most ancient god, the most venerable, and that he has the greatest anteriority when it is a question of acquiring virtue and happiness for humans" (180c).

So the most ancient god, the source of virtue and happiness, was the god of non-conflictual, positive relations, of the love which binds humans together so magically that they are prepared to die for one another. Eros is love and relation, the interdividual connection whereby each one of us owes everything to the other and only exists in that bond. Eros is the god of successful alterity.

Eryximachus speaks of the doctor, whose role is to reconcile contraries, to unite whatever separates, as opposed to Eros, which connects:

The practitioner . . . must be able to reconcile the jarring elements of the body and force them, as it were, to fall in love with one another. Now we know that the most hostile elements are the opposites, hot and cold, sweet and sour, wet and dry, and so on—and if, as I do myself, we are to believe these poets of ours, it was his skill in imposing love and concord upon these opposites that enabled our illustrious progenitor Asclepius to found the science of medicine. (186d–e)

Music is based on the same principle, quoting Heraclitus on this score: "The one in conflict with itself is held together, like the harmony of the bow and the lyre" (187a). Music, which creates harmony, is bound up with love. The interdividual relation must be loving, harmonious, devoid of any trace of rivalry, which is the source of conflicts as well as illness. Yet again in *The Symposium* (189d), Plato recounts the genesis of human beings. It is Aristophanes, the great comic poet of Greece, who is speaking:

> For in the beginning we were nothing like we are now. For one thing the race was divided into three: that is to say, besides the two sexes, male and female, which we have at present, there was a third which partook of the nature of both, and for which we still have a name though the creature itself is forgotten. For though "hermaphrodite'" is only used nowadays as a term of contempt, there really was a man-woman in those days, a being which is half male and half female. . . . And each of these beings was globular in shape, with rounded back and sides, four arms and four legs and two faces both the same on a cylindrical neck with one face one side and one the other, and four ears, and two sets of privates and all the other parts to match. (189e–190a)

These androgynes, we are told, were formidable: "And such, gentlemen, were their strength and energy and such their arrogance, that they actually tried . . . to scale the heights of heaven and set upon the gods" (190b). They are heading for what we read about in Genesis 3; they can remind us of the venom the serpent injected in Eve: "If you eat of this fruit, you will become like gods." The process is the same.

In *Symposium*, Zeus decides to weaken these impulses and make them human by cutting them in half: "And as each half was ready he told Apollo to turn its face, with the neck that was left, toward the side that was cut away . . . and then to heal the whole thing up" (190e). We read further on that "Zeus felt so sorry for them that he devised another scheme. He moved their privates around to the front . . . and made them propagate themselves, the male begetting upon the female" (191c).

Thus, for the Greeks, mimetic rivalry and violence are at the very outset consubstantial with being human. The rival and inordinate desire, called "hubris," drives the androgynes to mount an assault on the gods and Zeus, who reacts by dividing them in two, thus creating two "Alter" equals, one masculine and the other feminine, whose efforts will henceforth be aimed at being reunited.

Ever since then, the incomplete human being suffers, we might say, from reminiscences. Aristophanes continues:

> So you see gentlemen as far back we can trace our innate love for one another and how this love is always trying to reintegrate our former nature, to make two into one, and to bridge the gulf between one human being and another. . . . And so when . . . any lover is fortunate enough to meet his other half, they are both so intoxicated with affection, with friendship and with love that they cannot bear to let each other out of sight for a single instant. . . . And so all this to-do is a relic of that original state of ours, when we were whole and now, when we are longing for and following after that primeval wholeness, we say we are in love. (191c–193a)

Love, then, is the search for that complementary alterity that restores our original unity, our totality. In French, we often refer to our spouse as our moiety, and in English we speak of "my better half." Once reunited, these two moieties can no longer bear their separation. As a result of any sort of incident, their separation constitutes the woof and the weft of literature, and their final reunion is the "happy end." The suffering from separation is encapsulated by Lamartine's lovelorn eulogy: "One being is absent to you and all is empty" (*Un seul être vous manque et tout est dépeuplé*).

Thus Greek myth displays numerous resemblances with the text of Genesis 3. God created Eve by taking a rib from Adam and sewing up his wound. Certain exegetes translate Adam's rib as his "side," but the process reprises what Zeus does, with an enormous difference nonetheless: Zeus punishes the androgyne for its pride, its mimetic desire to depose the gods, whereas God creates Eve in order to complete Adam; she is to be a helpmate, lest he remain alone. Original sin, in the two myths, results from the same principle: rivalrous mimetic desire that spurs the androgynes to attack the gods, and this same desire injected into Eve by the serpent to become like the gods. Disobedience consists in appropriating the object that the model reserves for himself, an object considered to grant access to the very being of the model. This psychological process, this application of mimetic desire, is the founding and ubiquitous principle of the advertising industry.

We have just reviewed several centuries of the history of alterity. We now know that our symptoms, our syndromes, or mental illnesses are not due to the caprices of an intra-physical other, of sex organs endowed with a life that is "proper" to them. Nonetheless, to say that sexual frustration can lead to disorders affecting one's mood or behavior has become common knowledge. To say that sexuality is the driver of amorous passion, and therefore of monstrous jealous passions, is equally evident. We also now know that mental disorders are not caused by an extra-psychic other. The devil and demons have gone out of fashion. Demonic possession had its glory days with the Loudon possession episode, and these days witches do not have to fear the inquisitor's stake. Nonetheless, numerous victims continue to die from the blows of Islamic radicals, who accuse them of being unbelievers in Allah, and so of not respecting his law, and consequently of being in the grip of Satan.

Numerous colleagues still think, with Freud, that our neuroses are due to the agency of an intra-psychic other: the unconscious, which is held to be tightly linked to sexuality, as if concurring with theories of antiquity. I have long given up on that theory. First of all, because it involves multiple forms of alterity: the id, the super ego, Eros, Thanatos; it is the idea that we are the plaything of inner struggles between different agencies in the way that, for the Greeks, human destiny was the result of wars between the gods who were against us and those who protected us.

In our time, I have found in the research of certain quantum physicists new reasons to avoid the notion of the unconscious. Indeed, certain eminent researchers in this science think that consciousness is only the actualized reflection of a radical alterity, of a universal cosmic consciousness. The human brain, then, would no longer be the producer but rather the receptor of this consciousness, in the way that a radio produces nothing, but rather captures emissions coming from elsewhere. In Jean Staune's *Notre expérience a-t-elle un sens?*, we read:

Obviously consciousness is modified when certain regions of the brain are activated, but this idea does not prove that the brain produces consciousness any more than the idea that music is modified when we change the components of radio proves that the radio produces the music. Some neurologists do not hesitate to consider the brain as the condition and not as the ultimate cause of consciousness. (378)

In quantum physics, observation modifies the object of observation. An electron upon observation as a particle can become a wave. With memory, the observer in psychotherapy, which is to say the patient, the actual narrator, modifies, by observation and recollection, the nature of past events and feelings. At a pragmatic level, when speaking of a rival, toxic, pathogenic alterity, I have preferred, along with René Girard, using the word "misrecognition" [*méconnaissance*]. This has two advantages: the first is to highlight the active process at work in misrecognizing a toxic alterity; the second is to offer a therapeutic solution to mental distresses through the recognition of the toxic, rival alterity. This approach is wide-ranging and always the same; in this sense, it can be qualified as objective or scientific.

This is another difference from psychoanalysis, where everything depends upon interpretation. Paul Ricoeur has devoted two important works to interpretation and the conflicts about it, where he shows that the interpretations of the analysand and of the analyst are subjective. The recognition I endorse is often a difficult process, but it consists in a more complete therapeutic program: to lead the patient to face up to reality, to accept it, and recognize it for what it is, without any censure whatsoever, be it moral, ethical, political, ideological, cultural, emotional, or other. It is a therapy proposed by a psychology that is mimetic, relational, and interdividual.

As a matter of fact, this program holds for medical practice in general. Over the course of recent history infectious diseases have been identified by medical science as caused by pathogenic agents, viral or bacterial; in other words, by a toxic alterity that has invaded the organism, and whose detection and destruction is the task of white blood cells. Pasteur discovered that, by vaccination, one can induce these white blood cells to detect and combat these intruders. Immunotherapy stands today as a hope against all sorts of diseases, which consists in leading the white blood cells to first recognize the pathogenic alterity of certain cells and to destroy them.

To sum up, Culture has for centuries aimed at concealing the rival alterity, the real pathogen, under various disguises: of an intra-physical Other, of an extra-psychic Other, as an intra-psychic Other. The trend has always been to avoid recognizing the alterity of desire and, at the same time, to deny any responsibility for this desire that the "self" claims as its own. Culture is beginning to forsake every invention of a mythic alterity and to line up with René Girard's hypothesis of a mimetic desire mapped onto that of a very real other.

By contrast, neurosis and psychosis have in their own way reprised the concealment of pathogenic alterities described throughout history: the physical alterity for the Greek doctors for neuroses as arising from somatizations; and the psychic alterities of the Middle Ages for psychoses, by hallucinating the influence and action-at-a-distance of occult powers, demonic or statist (KGB, CIA), even extraterrestrial.

VII

The Clinical Reality of Alterity

I f we can abandon certain theories of pathogenic alterity and criticize them, the patients, for their part, in and by their symptoms, continue to represent a pathogenic alterity that is in their eyes responsible for their suffering. In hysterical neurosis, we have seen the case of a patient who concealed behind physical phenomena her inability to recognize the pathogenic rivalry that had infiltrated, insinuated itself, between her and her husband. The physical symptom is generated and invoked to dissimulate the rival alterity.

In neuroses of conversion, this is quite obvious: "My arm no longer obeys me, I cannot control it, that is the cause of my illness," or "I can no longer walk or get out of bed. That is the core of my illness. My legs get out of control, so I cannot move when I am in bed." We call this "astasia-abasia." In the same way, in certain psychoses, the patient otherizes a part of her psyche or her body to conceal the reality of a pathogenic alterity that is unbearable to recognize. Thus, in dysmorphophobia (one of the symptoms of schizophrenia, and sometimes only at the outset), the patient makes the form of his nose or ears responsible for all of his problems. In such a distorted view, cosmetic surgery would suffice to correct the problem. In this way, a physical detail is otherized and rejected as alien to the person. This excision would solve the problem. Cosmetic surgeons are well aware of these phenomena and rightly refuse to operate on these patients, despite their insistence, unless they have consulted a psychiatrist.

Finally, in numerous psychoses, the patient will otherize part of his or her psyche in the form of hallucinations, most often auditory, but also olfactive and kinesthetic. The real pathogenic alterity is hidden by the symptom: "The ones who persecute and insult me, I know who they are. It is they who make me suffer. Perhaps it is the CIA, the KGB, or such another organization."

In some cases, we can help this kind of patient. One day I was introduced to a sixteen-year-old girl, Amalia, whose parents were acquaintances of mine. They were very distraught, because Amalia "was hearing voices" and some doctors whom they consulted spoke of schizophrenia. Amalia wished to speak to me in the absence of her parents. I asked her: "I am told you are hearing voices."

Her answer: "No, I hear one voice."

"Do you recognize this voice? Is it the voice of someone you know?"

"No, but I have identified it. I recognize it. I have even given it a name."

"Oh? What name have you given it?"

"Alter."

I was flabbergasted, because that was the first time in my fifty-year career that I heard someone name alterity, so I asked her: "And you have conversations with Alter?"

"Yes. Sometimes we argue. Sometimes, he chews me out. Sometimes he consoles me when I am sad. I discuss everything with him very freely. That is why I call him my alter ego."

"In sum, instead of reflecting and talking to yourself about yourself, you talk to Alter."

"Yes. He at least answers me, because he understands me."

"May I give you some advice? Try to think on your own, to talk to yourself. Perhaps you will be able to understand yourself still better, or in any case, as well as Alter understands you."

She answers: "I am willing to try, but don't tell my parents."

I only tell the parents one thing: "Your daughter is not schizophrenic." I thought, in fact, and further developments confirmed this, that the recognition of an alterity at once friend and enemy, accomplice and critic, model and rival, was a step toward recognizing reality, the difficulty of her relations with others, and that her quasi-deliberate, hallucinated alterity was surely an original way, but not in the least crazy, of creating a friend and confidant whom she could also bawl out.

I would like to add here some quotations drawn from the archives of an eminent psychoanalyst, a friend of mine, Dr H. He divulged the files of some of his patients along with his observations, rightly thinking that some of these sessions would resonate with my concerns and research on alterity.

First case: In speaking of his work, an artist declares: "It is my creation, but it was effortless. This is wiretapping. My images are not my images, my music is not my music; it is as if someone has written it for me." In his notes, the psychoanalyst comments as follows: "The patient, a painter, feels like she is somehow inhabited. She observes an Other creating without effort. She is star gazing at this Other's art works."

Second case: I am struck by the psychoanalyst's note: "The majority of dreams take the form of a scenario redolent with character and roles, as in a theater." And he quotes and comments on the dream of his patient, who says: "I am a field of wheat. I move forward. There is only me. Me?" Thereupon the psychoanalyst asks his patient to engage in a free association, and she answers: "It is as if I were being shown the basic outline of my life." The psychoanalyst's notes include this personal comment: "This dreamer correctly registers her sense of her individual 'self' apart from the entity called the 'Selfhood.'"

Third case: A dream: "I wonder what I am. I have the wrong life." From an association of ideas we have: "Every one is the bearer of the whole. That is what is essential: the interaction with others."

Fourth case: A dream: "I had been on the phone with P. Then E. They both told me that I had been and would remain the woman of his life." Association of ideas: "I think that I am a muse. Energy? Magnetic energy? Everyone says, 'My life is better with you.'" To the psychoanalyst's question about this, the patient adds: "When I speak of being a muse, I don't mean myself, it is a mythification of me. . . . It is a magnetism which is not me." In his notes, the psychoanalyst adds the following comment: "The patient perceives herself as inhabited by an energy which is not she. In this case, others are fascinated by a symbolic representation of herself that she does not understand." And he adds: "This falls into the category of observations under the rubric: 'This is not only me.'"

Fifth case: The young woman on the couch declares her "surprise at the effect she has on those around her." Encouraged by the psychoanalyst to engage in free association, the patient declares: "It is like a dream. Somewhere there is a character imposed on me who is not me. I am the vector of a creation. . . . I am a spokesperson. It is not me that I saw. I did not see myself in what is separate from me. . . . Me! Me! The spokesperson of what is not me." The comments of the psychoanalyst are very revealing: "The patient is conscious of being inhabited. . . . She sees an ecstasy imposed upon her, a state in which she finds herself transported out of herself. . . . The ecstasy compels her to be only a semi-conscious vector whose role is to maintain the purity of the creation that goes through her." I would add a personal remark: to be in *ex-stasy* is to hold one's self out of one's self: to double one's self in a certain way that I would call *self-otherizing*. The psychoanalyst adds in his notes: "One notices the parallel with the piercing of Saint Theresa of Avila," whom he quotes as follows: "I would like to know how to explain . . . the difference that exists between being one and being ravished, where the elevation or flight of the spirit, the rapture is all the same. I am saying that the different words name the same thing and we call that *ecstasy*."

We find here the expression that I have just focused on. Regarding the same patient, the psychoanalyst adds a note: "She sees herself as a spokesperson. The French '*porte-parole*' resonates with the *Logos* that is also translated as *Word*"—as in the "Word became flesh" in John's gospel.

———————————

How do we help patients to recognize the pathogenic alterity, the toxic rival? The first step consists in remembering that the rival or obstacle was at first the model and that the enormous difficulty here is owing to the fact that it is unthinkable to admit that this respected, venerated model can be transformed into a rival or an obstacle, a difficulty enhanced by the fact that the model can be a pathogenic rival sometimes and at others become once again the model. Whence a feeling of ambivalence that often affects human relationships. But we can see such matters inversely; in his film, *Beauty and the Beast*, Jean Cocteau makes this plain. The Beauty first sees the other as a beast, a monster, because she fears it. She thinks that it is an enemy, a tormentor, a rival, but gradually the relation changes. Alterity appears less and less threatening, and in the end, confidence arises, even love. The relation has modified the perception of alterity, and the beast is transformed into a beautiful, perfectly lovable young man. Love has produced a miracle: it has transfigured the beast into Prince Charming.

VIII

Alterity in Physical Medicine

I have already mentioned vaccination, which consists in injecting a weak dose of a foreign element, a toxic alterity (bacteria) in order to enable our leucocytes to recognize this noxious alterity and destroy it. The organism defends itself because it recognizes the alterity as antagonistic, dangerous, foreign, toxic.

In this regard, I was amazed to read what Professor David Khayat wrote in *Enquête vérité: Vous n'aurez plus jamais peur du cancer*, and I shall quote him at length:

> Certain cancerous cells, in order to evade detection and destruction by our lymphocytes, will conceal themselves. This is a mechanism of protection that leads me to a link with pregnancy. In fact, when a woman carries an infant in her womb, she tolerates it, although everything about it has a different identity from her own since half of its genetic identity comes from the father. Proof of this lies in the fact that when this child reaches adulthood, he cannot donate one of his kidneys to his mother, because the mother's lymphocytes would recognize it as foreign, as "not self," and would reject it. (22–23)

There is, then, during pregnancy, a mysterious mechanism that allows for this feto-maternal "tolerance," a mechanism the allows the mother's organism to conceal the alterity that inhabits it. Khayat again: "During the nine months of pregnancy, a protein called HLA-G secretes and blocks the mother's immune system in order to prevent rejection of the fetus. Toward the end of the ninth month, the secretion of this protein begins to diminish and vanishes, activating childbirth, which is nothing less that the rejection of a foreign body," a body whose alterity is finally recognized and must be expelled. He continues: "The cancerous cells are capable of secreting this same HLA-G protein, thus inhibiting the lymphocytes, as if it were an embryo and not a tumor." The cells conceal their alterity, allowing the cancer to develop.

We are beginning to understand that health depends on the capacity of an organism to recognize toxic alterity and destroy it. I think that the same thing goes for the psyche. Neuroses and psychoses are mechanisms that misrecognize a rival alterity that is toxic, antagonistic; we call them mental illnesses because they are mistaken about who the real antagonist is, they instead create a substitute for the unrecognized antagonist, a scapegoat represented by an otherizing of a part of their physical or mental organism.

The recognition, the detection, the diagnosis of the dangerous alterity is therefore the key to health. About which David Khayat adds:

> The organism, in a kind of premonition of the danger that cancer represents for humanity, has developed a special immunizing control, uniquely aimed at hunting down cancerous cells. And there is a second system that calls on lymphocytes whose natural function is to identify and kill cancerous cells. These are called *Natural Killers*. Once activated, these NK lymphocytes can recognize cancerous cells by their tiniest differences. They do not need for them to be pointed out nor primed in order to kill them. They recognize them immediately and spontaneously.

In France, cancer attacks fifty percent of males and more than thirty percent of women, which prompted the oncologist to ask: "What triggers cancer and how?" This is where the oncologist and the psychiatrist meet: "Are stress and other violent emotions guilty of the onset of cancer, and if so, how?" He adds: "Stress consists in the ensemble of mental, emotional, and physical responses of the organism to aggravations and pressures. Its response always depends on the individual's perception of the pressures he or she is suffering from" (99–100).

What David Khayat calls "perception" is what I call "recognition of the origin of the stress in a rival, toxic alterity." The subject has to put up with this frustration for all sorts of reasons: ethical, religious, economic, affective, familial, etc. After asking the patient: "What are you suffering from?" I advise my students to ask him or her, "Whom are you suffering from?" and to consider the answers as so many excuses for the misrecognition.

The recognition of a rival alterity, the identification of the toxicity of such relations, is very difficult because the process extends over several years. A cancer takes time to develop, and the same goes for a neurosis or a psychosis. David Khayat rightly emphasizes the difficulty, not to say impossibility, of retrospective examination. And he concludes: "This obstacle to retrospective reckoning makes it difficult to shed light on the psychogenesis of cancer" (208).

The same difficulty arises in psychiatry. Freud was faced with it when he directed psychoanalysis toward the earliest stages of life. But he came up against a difficulty that he could not foresee. Psychoanalysis focuses on memory, on recollection. But as I have shown in *The Puppet of Desire* and *The Mimetic Brain*, human relations are governed by the laws of Newtonian physics, while memory phenomena appear to obey the laws of quantum physics. In our memory, we can in effect go back in time and find ourselves simultaneously in two different places or time periods. It is especially in quantum physics that we concede that the future or the present can influence or modify the past. An active, toxic misrecognition can therefore modify past events at will in order to explain or justify an imperviousness, an opacity to understanding.

Stress, as described by Hans Selye in *The Stress of Life*, triggers two types of responses: fight or flight. In my view, acute stress can be found at the origin of cancers as well as mental illnesses in a situation where neither solution is possible. Here is a person dear to you, who suffers, who poisons your life, because you cannot quit the relation nor fight against it. You are cornered, a prisoner of your affective ties, of your feelings, of your education, of your religious convictions. One of my patients, whose husband adored her, was suddenly taken ill, unable to move, barely able to speak. She expressed her consternation and her feeling of being imprisoned and helpless: "I can no longer live with him, but neither can I live without him." These insoluble situations strike me as the height of stress, as super-stress, a "checkmate" that life metes out, and from which the only outcome is physical or mental illness. To characterize this checkmate feeling, American practitioners have come up with the concept of "hopelessness, helplessness."

On this topic, David Khayat recounts the experiments conducted on rats that were subjected to various stresses, and he concludes: "The animal that can react by fight (experiment 1) or by flight (experiment 2) does not develop organic problems. The animal that can neither flee nor fight (experiment 3) is blocked and exhibits pathological disturbances." In psychiatry, when the rival alterity can be neither contested nor escaped, it is transformed into a radical alterity that shatters the "self"; the outcome is either utter powerlessness or a violence turned against oneself. This chronic frustration lies at the source of all sorts of depressions and neuroses, often as utter submission, leading gradually to complete self-effacement or self-destruction, for example, in the form of cancer or suicide.

To summarize: in physical medicine, all infectious illnesses are due to the irruption of a rival alterity, a toxic and aggressive other in the organism: bacterial, viral, fungal, etc. We have medicines (antibiotics, antivirals, anti-fungals) to defend us against them. We ingest an alterity as an ally to eliminate the enemy alterity. We have also discovered vaccines, which consist in reinforcing white blood cells that protect us. We inject a weak dosage of this enemy and our leucocytes learn to recognize and destroy it. We are thereby immunized against the illness in question.

As to cancer, David Khayat informs us that our inability to combat the illness is due to the inaptitude of our leucocytes to recognize and identify cancerous cells that are concealed behind a camouflaged enzyme. The essence of the illness seems to be linked to the mutation of cells in the organism into an aggressive alterity that is toxic, pathogenic; the cancerous cell's development is anarchic, invasive, and destructive. But Khayat also tells us that the origin of this "metamorphosis" of a normal cell into a cancerous one, this destructive *otherizing*, can be due to a host of toxic factors: tobacco, nutrition, environment, virus, etc. He adds that stress enhances cancer mortality and concludes that it is "the inability to adequately manage the stress that is the origin of that impact. The effect of stress on the progress of the cancer is clearly linked to our inability to bear it or manage it." (126) It is fair to ask if stress stymies the recognition by leucocytes of their former allies become mortal enemies.

In psychiatry, I have explained at length in *The Mimetic Brain* that the other can fill a variety of roles:

- A model: a friend, an associate, a confederate, our best friend, our spouse, our colleague, our partner, etc. In this case, everything he or she does is good. We have the same tastes; decisions and choices from this person are habitually welcome.
- A rival. This same model, this same other, can be transformed; the alliance relation turns into confrontation. As Girard has shown in the works of Shakespeare, the best friends become the worst enemies when mimetic desire leads them to focus on the same object: the same woman, the same position, any object that cannot be shared. As I myself have insisted in *The Genesis of Desire* about even the most harmonious, loving couples, the discord arises from mimetic desire bearing on an object that cannot be shared in any way—power, for instance. It is the same for politics. The friendly alterity that has metamorphosed into a rival alterity brings on terrific stress with devastating physiological consequences, but the worst can be avoided if one can recognize this transformation clearly, the changed reality of the relation, and reserve the right to the possibility of "fight or flight": oppose this other who has become a rival or avoid this person.
- But if one does not succeed in recognizing the metamorphosis of alterity from model to rival, if one suffers from this violent tension without being able to escape or oppose it for the simple reason that one misrecognizes it, this rival becomes an obstacle that is impossible to evade or destroy. I wish to underline the fact that this other is still the same, that it is the relation to him or her that has changed. The mechanisms of mimetic rivalry change the positive relation into an obstacle relation. I insist as well that it is the misrecognition of this metamorphosis, the illusory belief that the model is still a model, whereas in fact this person has become a rival and obstacle, that causes various psychiatric and psychopathological disorders, and, according

to David Khayat, accounts for the failure of the organism to combat cancer.

Thus, the only way an organism, in its physical or psychic dimension, can sustain and defend itself is to clearly recognize reality for what it is, and not persist in generating techniques and mechanisms that misrecognize the toxic and pathogenic alterity.

Autoimmune diseases provide another example of the pathogenic transformation of a friend into an enemy, of a model into a rival. In this case, the leucocytes, misled by complex mechanisms that I cannot explain here, brusquely take their sister cells, those of their own organism, for enemies, and attack them, destroy them, causing serious illness. Autoimmune diseases are a triumph of misrecognition.

These two kinds of disease exhibit the very same misrecognition of reality. With cancer, an alterity that has become a rival and enemy is not recognized as such because it conceals the transformation behind various guises that are too complicated to explain here. In autoimmune diseases, the friendly alterity is mistaken as hostile and attacked. We find this double misprision all the time in psychopathology; the misrecognition of the alterity as model or rival is the source of many problems. In psychopathology, alterity can be taken as model, as rival, or as obstacle.

This is why, in psychopathology, as in physical medicine, we must not mistake the adversary if we wish to avoid serious problems, as I have emphasized in *The Genesis of Desire*, as Jacques Luccesi has done in *Le Désir d'être un autre*, and Girard in his book on Dostoevsky. Our difficulty here derives from the fact that the model, friend, or accomplice and the rival, toxic, enemy, and insurmountable obstacle are one and the same person. It is not the Other who changes, it is the relation to the Other. Hence the need to elaborate a relational and interdividual psychopathology and psychotherapy, focused on recognizing the transformation of the friend relation into a rival relation that is jealous, envious; and recognizing this transformation into a relation of antagonism, resulting in a mental block, an impasse.

IX.

Mimetic Psychotherapy

Illnesses and Problems

H ow can we recognize the metamorphoses of alterity and detect the interplay of mimetic desire?

I have emphasized the temptation of misrecognition in the realm of physiology and psychology and its pathogenic and destructive effects, whatever the mechanisms that activate it. I now turn to focus only on psychopathology. In *The Mimetic Brain*, I argue that the essential mechanism of misrecognition of the other in his or her metamorphoses into rival and obstacle consists in otherizing a somatic or mental region, leading to neurosis or psychosis. This otherizing favors the creation of a factitious culprit, whose role is to dissimulate certain realities, and to take the place of the real other as a model that has become rival or obstacle.

The mechanism at work is comparable to that of the scapegoat as described by René Girard. In order to dispel violence and avoid confrontation, we accuse a third party, chosen at random, as responsible for all disorders. Its otherizing, its expulsion from the community, is assumed to restore peace. This emissary victim is branded as guilty because he or she has been accused. This mechanism is clearly pathological on the individual level, even if it proves salutary on the social level, because it relies on a lie, a falsification of reality. The victim is guilty because of the accusation, whereas if we stick to reality and to truth, we could only accuse and condemn if the guilt is proven. We must only accuse the guilty.

How does it happen that the same mechanism, the same fraud, produces positive effects on the social level by restoring peace to the community, and generates pathogenic stalemates when it is triggered in the individual psyche? Because in psychopathology, it is easy to create a physical or mental alterity and to blame it as the culprit, but it is impossible to expel it. The only salutary, therapeutic solution is therefore to recognize the mechanism for what is, namely, a displacement or evasion, a "conversion" and otherizing of a body part, an organ, or motor or sensorial function, and blame it for the pathology. Consequently, mimetic psychotherapy will endeavor to expose the misrecognition, to deconstruct it, and reveal the mechanisms at work that spring from a fear to face up to reality, namely, the monstrous transformation of the other.

This transformation of the other as model into the other as rival or as obstacle is not inflexible or unchangeable. It fluctuates, evolves, changes according to the circumstances and the variable geometry of the interdividual relation. It is this flexibility that makes the recognition of the toxic alterity so difficult. It is not stable. Evolutions, changes, backsliding are always possible. So it is that the misrecognition always finds excuses by representing different episodes of the interdividual relation.

At this stage of deliberation, I can only refer the reader to *The Mimetic Brain* concerning psychopathology and a new nosology and classification of mental illnesses. But for those interested in everyday psychology, we have to acknowledge at all times that neither psychology nor psychotherapy concern only illnesses; in ordinary consultations, they address *problems* that we can also call symptoms and syndromes. It is the latter that I wish to focus on here. All the problems that lead people to consult a therapist, a psychoanalyst, a seer, a guru, or religious adviser have to do with a relation to another or others, to an alterity that is real and identified or to a built-in alterity in the form of moral laws or rules—what Freud called the superego. The absence of an explicit scapegoating otherizing, neurotic or psychotic, makes the toxicity of this alterity especially difficult to accept. Whence the problem of how to help the patient to identify and recognize the toxic alterity without casting blame upon it, attacking it, or trying to destroy it. To console the patient's inability to do this, and find solutions to the problem, is an art that concerns psychology no less than politics.

I can illustrate my point by the following anecdote, related to me by a brilliant young engineer. He was madly in love with a woman slightly older than he, who was divorced and the mother of a little girl. This was his first emotional sexual experience, and it made him happy. Learning about this liaison, his father, on the other hand, argued against it on logical grounds: "You are too young and this will interrupt your studies. You cannot, at your age, take on a child, who, what's more, is not your own." The engineer told me he had had long conversations, sometimes stormy, with his father, and that he had used an expression that amused his father and enabled them to laugh together and to tone down the dispute. The son had said: "Listen, what you see as a problem is a solution for me." His father saw the woman as a source of problems, which was objectively true, but his son emphasized the immediate and very physical benefits of that relationship.

Alterity from Day to Day

In everyday life, toxic, pathogenic alterity is difficult to identify or recognize because it is changeable, fluctuating, flexible; it is constantly being modified from one day to another, from one situation to another. Culture at large has long had great difficulty in recognizing toxic alterity because of the neuroses and psychoses aiming to conceal it by activating pathological otherizing, physical or mental, depending on whether neurotic or psychotic mechanisms were involved.

In the psychopathology of everyday life, the symptoms of distress are undifferentiated, multiple, variable for only one reason: the model is constantly transformed into a rival or an obstacle and goes back to being a model and friend, whence the unspecified symptoms that show up in everyday life; they are diverse and changing at the whim of multiple metamorphoses of the other, who appears alternately and successively now as the friend, ally, partner, and then as aggressive, irritating, toxic rival. This killjoy or spoilsport is always throwing a spike in the wheels, not doing what we want and all the while preventing us from doing it ourselves. I am speaking here of manifestations and isolated syndromes that are not integral to a specified neurotic or psychotic pathology.

Guilt

In my view, there are two kinds of guilt: one that is only triggered by the discovery of wrongdoing or misconduct and the other that requires complex discernment.

This is a guilt that inhibits every action, the agency that Freud baptized as the superego and that in France we call the "principle of precaution," the successor to what, for centuries, was the result of "an examination of conscience." The superego prohibits acts and even thoughts, while the principle of precaution prohibits any act or behavior that is likely to involve risk. The superego is individual and particular, according to one's education, culture, religion, etc. The principle of precaution is universal; its prohibitions apply to everyone, which is absurd since life itself is risk.

In both cases, guilt is wrangling with responsibility: wrongdoing or blunder in the first case and avoidance of any action that can lead to culpable responsibility in the second case. In the first case, responsibility is attenuated, seeking resolution in denials, lies, excuses. On the legal level, it can lead to a trial that allows the accused to outsource guilt, confiding one's determination as much as possible to one's lawyers. On the individual level, this kind of problem can require a psychologist instead of the courtroom. This is the case of one spouse discovering the infidelity of the other. A process of accusation and guilt is activated on one side, of resentment and frustration on the other. This situation can end by divorce or the effort for a solution with the help of a professional, who will ask the unfaithful partner to face reality, without reticence or guilt. What does he or she truly want? What is the real desire? Return to the spouse or go off with the other? Once that reality is clearly established and identified, one can address the injured spouse, either to console or bring about forgiveness. In both cases, it is necessary for this person to face reality without dodging or excusing it. This involves two options:

- Recognize the transformation of the model into a rival and abandon the struggle, with its conflicts, in the interest of self-preservation, in order to go on with life: *flight*, divorce or separation.

• Accept that the rival should become again a model, which amounts to forgiving him or her, but without humiliating this person or bringing up the infidelity on every occasion. The point is to prevent the conflict from being a chronic condition by constantly reverting to fault-finding. In *The Mimetic Brain*, I reported the case of the wife whom I had advised to work supportively with her husband in order to restore peace to the household.

In the case where the patient is tormented by his or her superego, it is necessary here again to face reality: accept one's guilty feelings, evaluate them, measure the consequences if acted upon, and recognize their origin in the mechanisms of mimetic desire, where the other appears sometimes as model, sometimes as rival, and sometimes as obstacle, at the whim of the least fluctuations in the interdividual relation.

To clearly recognize the reality of our most secret, most "guilty" desires, is to demystify them and remove their anxiety prone character, if only because once we have shared them with the therapist, who is neither horrified nor shocked, but instead invites us to understand and analyze and accept this desire as well as its nonfulfillment. The trap to avoid is the temptation to place blame on the other, the spouse, for example. Distress and anxiety are produced by the wrongdoing because the superego is unforgiving.

This was the case of a fifty-year-old who consulted me, saying: "Something frightful, startling, unthinkable has happened to me: I cheated on my wife." My logical question is: "Are we talking about a fling, a drunken party, or about an affair?" He answers, "A fling, a drunken party. I lost my self-control." "And what did you do next?" I asked. "I immediately confessed to my wife, and I am depressed, because that made her very unhappy." So, I replied, "Why did you tell your wife?" And he: "Because I am honest!"

After a few moments of silence because I had to calm my irritation and refrain from getting angry, I finally said to him, "Face up to reality. You have not been able to deal with your guilt. You decided instead to put the burden on your wife. That reflects a weakness that we have to work on. Because this has nothing to do with honesty. Your wife is distraught, torn between resentment and guilt that you have passed on to her, who is asking herself if her husband's behavior is her fault: 'What has he to reproach me for? What have I done or not done?'"

I conclude by telling him that we have work to do, that I am ready to see his wife as well, and that the solution to the arrival of this unforeseen rival demands time and effort to resolve the problem. In fact, his confession had brusquely made of him a rival in the eyes of his wife, who had suddenly lost confidence in him and in herself. The goal of psychotherapy is to show to each one that the perfect model, friend, lover, beloved, can at any moment be transformed into an alien rival, distant and hostile, and that the solution for both of them consists in facing reality and accepting it as being part of life and its inevitable fluctuations in the interdividual relation. I conclude about guilt here with a remark of Girard, who said of Dostoyevsky, "He was strong enough face up to his weaknesses. He is too weak to forgive them in himself." The patient, too weak to forgive himself, transferred that burden to his wife.

Comparison

This is the basic mechanism that subtends mimetic desire; it involves the difference between what I have or what I am and what the other has or is. This difference is only inferred by comparison.

It is in endless relation to the other that I exist, that I situate and evaluate myself, and take the measure of my belongings, my happiness, my very existence. Comparison is consequently a basic mechanism, essential and dangerous, and I have evoked its role on the matter of "original sin" and human origins in *The Genesis of Desire*. As Jacques Luccesi writes: "We cannot exaggerate the poison that comparison introduces into our lives." It is a poison that is at the same time a remedy, like the Greek *pharmakon* studied by Derrida in "Plato's Pharmacy," and it is a poison represented by alterity, which is how we evaluate our existence. As Girard writes of Raskolnikov, the protagonist in *Crime and Punishment:* "Raskolnikov does not know if his solitude makes him superior or inferior to others, an individual-god or an individual-worm, and the Other remains the arbiter of this debate. Raskolnikov always depends on the other's verdict about what he is" (Girard 2012, 29).

Mimetic reciprocity is skewed. The gaze that I direct at the other is a comparison, the one he or she directs at me is a judgment. In *The Gambler*, Dostoyevsky stages this reciprocity, and Girard says of it: "It is the consciousness of being gazed upon by the young woman that counts for everything in the eyes of this new underground character" (30–31). But the interdividual relation changes, evolves; it is never stable. Girard proposes an illuminating comparison to this character by alluding to Marivaux's theatrical masterpiece, *Le Jeu de l'amour et du hasard*: "The game of love is one with the game of chance" (31).

I might add that the same goes for the game of hate, of contempt, as well as of admiration. The relation to the other oscillates like a seesaw. On this "diabolical" interplay, if the Other is high, I am low. To me this is unbearable, but the only way for me to go up is to make the other go down by any means necessary according to the circumstances. This seesaw is "diabolical" because it is not possible that the Other go down on his own, nor can the Self go up unless the Other goes down. It is therefore vital for me to bring the Other down. The rivalry is impossible to resolve unless we change the game.

I and the other, at the whim of mimetic desires, of comparison and minute details, never stop going up and down, always in reverse relation to each other. When the movement of the seesaw speeds up, the images I have of the other, as either a god or demon, either high or low, end up by being confused cinematographically, and the other appears monstrous, terrifying, superior and inferior, god and devil at once. This situation is extreme; in ordinary clinical practice, the patient complains of varying feelings about the other; they fluctuate according to the behaviors, reactions, and attitudes of the other regarding him or her. This instability gnaws at the relation and threatens to escalate and snowball at any moment. We hear the woman say: "I don't recognize the man I loved," and he is humming like Charles Aznavour: "Come back again as the little girl who gave me so much happiness. . . . Don't go away, don't go away!" Comparison is permanently at work in time and space, in the present gaze and in memory, in behavior of the moment and in recollection. Mimetic psychotherapy aims to help the patient to see the reality of these changes without reacting with exaltation or discouragement. But it is very difficult for the patient to arrive at a fixed image of him- or herself, as little dependent as possible on the other's gaze. This difficulty explains the sadness besetting the couple and, at another level, the sociological discouragement preceding revolt or revolution. The class struggle aims at nothing less than recognition in the eyes of those who have more and are more than we. The solution is for everyone to get off the infernal seesaw.

Envy and Jealousy

Spinoza called envy and jealousy the "sick passions." They can remain mini-
mal and "benign," without escalating to a toxic, rivalrous intensity. If they
grow more powerful, they rank with the large group of rival passions that can
result in the most serious pathologies. Simply put, envy is the suffering that
comparison generates between what the other has or is and what I myself
have or am. Jealousy is the fear, perhaps even the phobia in a rivalrous sense
that I will shortly examine, of losing what I have, what belongs to me and
that the other seems to wish to take from me: my wife, my husband, my job,
or any of my possessions. The evil eye is reputed to be able to destroy even
my health.

As to envy, I cannot resist citing here some words of General de Gaulle
that Luc Ferry brought up in *Le Figaro* of July 25, 2019: "Envy is our national
vice. It is the worst of the capital sins, the one that sent the angels to hell
because they resented God for his superior being. . . . Envy is the feeling of
the vanquished and hate-mongers. It is the crime of Cain against Abel, of
the one who failed and kills his neighbor, because of the latter's success."
The psychological, sociological, and political remedy to envy is what Shakespeare's Ulysses called "degree," hierarchy, in *Troilus and Cressida*. Luc Ferry
continues:

> As Tocqueville has shown in *Democracy in America*, a society made up of
> separate orders is largely free of its sad passions, each one coming into his
> world, his compartment, his class or caste, without especially trying to leave
> it behind. As long as people think that hierarchy is a historical and natural
> truth, written into the order of things, they are not obsessed with the idea
> of getting free of it. . . . The situation is otherwise in the world of equality
> and human rights, according to which humans are born free and equal in
> rights. The powerful passion of envy is bound up with egalitarianism.

The fatal trap is to think that humans are not only born equal but that they
should be so *in everything*. It is the quest for a mythical, impossible uniformity that leads to myriad frustrations.

Thus envy, in its most extreme consequences, like the "pruning" of
aristocratic heads held too high during France's Reign of Terror, is always

justified by draping itself in the immaculate mantle of justice. Ferry quotes John Rawls's *Theory of justice* to this effect: "We can define envy as the tendency to experience hostility at the sight of others' greater wealth, even if their superior condition takes nothing away from our own advantages. We just want to deprive them of their privileges."

The envious person wishes above all to dispossess the other of what he or she lacks that the other possesses unjustly. Mimetic desire is the mechanism underlying envy and jealousy. The idea is that the other desires what I possess, seeks to take it from me, and I am jealous. The other has something that I do not and that I cannot have, so I can satisfy my mimetic rivalry by dispossessing this other of what he has, because I am envious. Envy and jealousy are sometimes conjoined. I can be jealous "about my wife" if I think that another has his eyes on her, but I can also be jealous of my wife herself if she shines more brightly in society, and then jealousy is transformed into envy. In *The Genesis of Desire*, I call these two types "jealousy of a third party and jealousy of my better half."

In everyday experience, comparison finds expression in envy and jealousy. Envy is the daughter of admiration in the drama of comparison. The other has non-negotiable qualities that I find lacking in me: beauty, intelligence, culture, savoir faire, wealth, and even luck. As Luccesi points out, "the envious person places himself straightaway on the plane of equality. He resents the lack that besets him or the inferiority of his situation as an injustice" (29). Envy can validate itself by demands of justice and equality. Alas, not everyone can have beauty, intelligence, wealth. The demand is going to devolve into the imperative to dispossess those with advantages over us in order that equality and justice may triumph. On the political level, such comparisons raise enormous problems that ideologies have failed to resolve to this day. In reality, the least detail, the least shimmer nourishes and justifies an envy that suspects every gesture, every attitude. In extreme cases, jealousy is no longer just a problem but a pathology, going as far as murder in the case of Othello. Jealousy can make us puppets ready to kill in order to deprive a rival of an object that eludes us. In Clouzot's film *La Vérité*, Brigitte Bardot shoots her lover when he tells her that he is leaving her for her sister. She kills him "literally" without knowing what she is doing. The character will plead a "crime of passion" all the while proclaiming her total love for her victim and her despair about an act that is incomprehensible to her.

Psychotic jealousy, rivalrous passion, prevail against love and any other feeling. In *Othello*, this passion is psychotic because the rival does not exist. Desdemona loves Othello, is faithful to him, is innocent. Nonetheless he kills her to ensure that she will belong to no one else, to defeat any potential rival. Othello does not suffer from envy: he does not covet what another could possess but develops an insane, psychotic jealousy because he fears that another could go off with his wife. His deed is psychotic because his rival is imaginary.

With Clouzot, the rival passion could be called neurotic because the rival exists: the character played by Bardot is the sister of Dominique, and her lover has just told her that it is for this person that he is leaving her. To forego the object of her desire is impossible to her, especially to the advantage of her sister. The rival desire, the rivalrous passion, prevails against love: the object of desire is destroyed so as not to belong to another—contrary to what the true mother will choose in the judgment of Solomon.

As I have written in a previous book, we are puppets of desire. Comparison spawns mimetic desire, and this often works on us against our will and our reason, even without our knowing it. In sum, jealousy oscillates at the whim of the smallest details. I recall the words of Nero in Racine's tragedy, *Britannicus*: "I understand glances that you think are mute."

With many couples, jealousy manifests itself in the guise of surveillance and questioning in the interest of love. This surveillance sparks distrust in the other, and mistrust sets in between them. Wanting endless reassurances to appease or ward off suspicions, the jealous person enlarges a distance and mistrust that can lead to a breakup or to an endless game of cat and mouse. This trap awaits not only "loving" couples but also friendships and all sorts of business gatherings and politics where power is at issue. In many traditions, jealousy and envy are expressed in terms of the evil eye. One fears the harmful consequences that could come about from the fact that one's neighbor regards with an "evil eye" my new car, my new coat, my recent promotion, etc. This widespread belief is an affiliate of superstition and can end up being verified by the ruses of self-fulfilling prophecy.

Love

Love is the central subject of literature worldwide, which shows its capital importance in the therapist's office, where the problems of love, hate, and unresponsiveness are brought up constantly; they present themselves in the clinical form of depression, discouragement, anger, rage, the desire for vengeance, doubts about oneself and the meaning of life. When one "falls in love," the love relation modifies the "self" as well as the other. Alterity is experienced as beneficial, almost miraculous. A constant wonderment sets in, and it brightens the whole world.

The "self" of desire evolves, becoming the self of the desire of the other, and, as Girard notes about Dostoyevsky's fiction: "The 'self' is not an object alongside with other objects. It is constituted by a relation to the other and we cannot consider it outside this relation" (*Resurrection*, 43). And so, in the love relation, a new "self" appears, constituted by its relation to the other that is enchanting, providential, miraculous. This new "self" will grow during the relation and will only exist in its relation to the other. This is why, when a breakup occurs, this new "self" goes through mortal anguish. In effect, a definitive breakup would mean the self's disappearance, its death. Henceforth, psychotherapy will have its hands full with this "self" in the process of dissolution, self-deprecation, and disparagement. This new "self" is going to disappear since the divinity that created it has departed and the bereft no longer deserves to live. The "self" that remains is nothing, and the devaluation can lead to suicide. Upon receiving the breakup letter from Valmont in *Dangerous Liaisons* and believing that he never loved her, Madame de Tourvel gives up on life.

The psychotherapist will be at great pains to desacralize the other and help the patient rebuild another "self." The task will be to appease and console the emotional brain and to reason with the cognitive brain; to express consideration for this "self" but not pity. It is a long-term task. In the words of a psychanalyst whose courses I have taken, "it is a big job, week by week."

Love only becomes passion when it encounters a rival; the queen of passions is the rivalrous passion, and rivalry is always triangular. Jealousy plays an essential role in the combustion of a rivalrous passion, and this can lead to all kinds of excess. There are crimes of passion, suicides of passion. The psychotherapist must endeavor to dispassionate the rivalry by finding other modes of expression for it, while getting help from the patient's entourage; if necessary, the therapist must resort to psychotropic drugs, such as tranquilizers, even hospitalization as a last extremity. The "griefs" of love are problems that must be taken very seriously. The psychotherapist must help in the mourning process of the "self" that has been destroyed and forever lost by the other's abandonment. It is this mourning of the self-of-desire of the other, the self created by the relation, the *self-between*, in the words of Eugene Webb, that requires attention. It is easier to mourn a deceased person than a living one whom one always imagines in the arms of a rival.

It is necessary to point out that love is much easier to give than to receive. The one who gives overflows with love poured out to the other. The one who receives may not be as amorous, or may feel obligated by it, even besieged by it, and it is difficult to accept that this love can be felt as invasive. Many couples are destroyed by this asymmetric alterity. Without wishing to indulge in theology, it is evident that if God is Love, his infinite Love is very difficult to accept for humans, for whom that love would "obligate."

To accept receiving another's love creates a kind of obligation, not to say a debt, for the receiver. In the interdividual relation, the giver finds him- or herself high on the diabolical seesaw. Suddenly, the receiver finds him- or herself automatically, inevitably low. One cannot help feeling uneasy and wishing to go up high. For this, there is only one possible means: bring the other down.

Such is the perverse effect of a great love. It begins with a rivalry about the intensity of the love itself:

"I love you madly."

"Me too."

"I adore you."

One soon runs out of superlatives. The matter shifts to proofs of love, and in clinical consultations, we hear reflections of this sort:

"He has just given me a superb, priceless necklace. Of course, he is richer than I, but this bothers me. Should I break up with my lover on this account?"

"She is hugely richer than I. She has just bailed out my business that was on the verge of bankruptcy, but who does she think she is?"

From then on, all means are good to lower the giver because gratitude is rare, as rare as true love. To lower the other, we hear nasty thoughts and observe quite unpleasant attitudes:

"You should change hairdressers; your hair looks awful . . ."

"Your necktie is ridiculous, which doesn't surprise me. It's one of the rare ones you chose for yourself."

"You need to lose weight. You eat too much, you drink too much, and what's more you smoke . . ."

And of course, there are lies, infidelities, and discourtesies, designed to persuade oneself that he or she is not a prisoner, is free, and if the other loves us so much, that is his or her problem.

It is obvious that the love relation in any form is closely involved with sexuality. What makes the relation human is the rivalry that infiltrates it to varying degrees. From the moment the serpent injected rivalry into Eve's mimetic desire, Adam and Eve became human. They left the world of Edenic paradise and entered the real world of time as we know it. Since then, every sexual relation would have a rivalrous, violent, aggressive component; in a normal amorous relation, it comes in homeopathic doses. It is nonetheless true that the love relation comprises a dimension of submission or domination; the cherished, beloved, adulated other is sometimes dominant, sometimes submissive.

Male orgasm can be interpreted as submission, surrender, in the amorous jousting. This can lead to premature ejaculation: the man gives up, concedes even before a struggle. Female orgasm is a surrender, a gift that she gives or does not. I have a patient who boasted that she was frigid because she said that warded off any dependence on the man, ensuring her freedom. Her partner was to submit to her, have an orgasm, and become dependent on her moods. I can also cite the case of that patient who was furious because the man she loved had found means to bring her to orgasm for the first time in her life, and who was afraid of becoming dependent. She hastened to cheat on him to avoid that catastrophe.

Rivalrous alterity in the interdividual relation of lovers is particularly flagrant in Don Juan types and their female counterpart as a famously wanton Messalina, as I argue in *The Mimetic Brain*. What advice can we give in mimetic psychotherapy to a man or woman in love? I think we must exclude any judgment about what the other is or has. The qualities of the other can be admirable and adorable but can become unbearable over time. In plain language, it is pointless to try to evaluate "objectively" the character and qualities of the other.

What is possible on the other hand is to evaluate the relation that has set in for the couple; to analyze the interdividual relation and detect the proportion of rivalry that inhabits it. The psychotherapist will then be able to help the patient face up to the reality, to accept it, and live with it. It is up to the patient to decide in full knowledge of the actual situation what he or she is ready to accept.

This process is especially relevant in the modern world. In traditional societies, the couple is held together, supported, and constrained, by the social group, the family, custom, religion, etc. None of these retaining walls exist today. For example, we can ask a simple question: "Do I feel proud to be going out with someone so attractive, so rich, so powerful? Or am I calm, serene, and happy when we are alone together?" To the question "what is a love relation that ends well?"—the answer is "a love relation that does not end."

Anxiety and Anguish

To varying degrees, these are a problem for everyone. Rarely do they not come up in a therapeutic relation. Anxiety and anguish are the most acute states of stress. This ranges from mere apprehensions and disquiet to a crisis accompanied by suffocation, chest pains, even fainting. There is always an element of alterity underlying stress that is stifling (agoraphobia); a friend or enemy alterity that supports me and whose absence can be acute (claustrophobia); an aggressive alterity (phobia of small animals, of viruses, of bacteria, of illness in general). Phobias that fasten on objects (knives, department stores, rats, etc.) can ward off stress by avoidance: *flight*. The displacement upon an object, a situation, an animal, an illness, only disguises the role of the other. These are so many ways by which reality is concealed; they can include otherizing a part of the body or the mind, which can trigger a neurosis or psychosis. This rival alterity shows up in the language of political correctness, which condemns for example, Islamophobia or homophobia. Here the conflictual relation with enemy, hated rivals concerns a real other, although quite anonymous, but who can at any moment be individualized and assaulted. Unalloyed anxiety and anguish can remind us of film scenarios where the character is terrorized by a menacing other that the spectator senses but without its being visualized. The screams of the terrorized character are alone evidence of the threatening alterity that does not appear but that the spectators surmise. Anguish arises to the level of paroxysm when no escape is possible. No *flight*, but neither the possibility of *fight*. At this point, anguish gives rise to panic.

It is amusing to see the therapeutics proposed for anxiety attacks. They range from a plastic bag over the face to increase the rate of carbon dioxide in the blood to ionic supplements to especially high doses of magnesium and extending to hormones and megavitamins. Mimetic psychotherapy will focus upstream on the toxic, pathogenic rival alterity that is misrecognized or outright denied. This is complicated, drawn out, and difficult but necessary if we wish to avoid increasing doses of tranquilizers.

Do These Problems Have Solutions?

To summarize: in our overview of the history of medicine and psychopathology, we have seen the rival and toxic alterity was assigned a physical, in-body locality. Later on, it was identified as something outside the psyche. Finally, Freud came along with the genius idea of lodging it in an intra-psychic otherness that is unconscious and acts on us without our knowing it; this allows for the ownership of desire while avoiding responsibility for its unconscious origin and its consequences. In the second half of the previous century, with the work of René Girard, of Andrew Meltzoff in child psychology, and the discovery of mirror neurons, we have seen the other revealed as the source of "my desires," which is thoroughly mimetic. This revelation is denied and rejected by a neurosis that persists in concealing the alterity by a somatic otherizing and by a psychosis that persists in otherizing part of the psyche for the same purpose.

But if Freud could develop some consistency in his research by affirming the reality of a neurotic or psychotic structure, subsequent research and practice have found these "structures" to be incomprehensible, irreparable, nonexistent. Concerning our current passions, contemporary psychopathology is characterized by a destructuration that gradually blurs the lines and contours of the structure. Whence the regularly updated American *Diagnostic and Statistical Manual of Mental Disorders* (*DSM*), which classifies clinical charts statistically by regrouping symptoms and disparate elements under hundreds of rubrics. I have remarked to my American colleagues that every human is in principle unique and that we cannot reduce pathological tendencies to some hundreds of symptoms, such that we would have to recognize seven billion different mental and psychopathological combinations.

These days, the Freudian structures are like a painting drenched with a bucket of water that is trickling down, allowing us here and there to perceive a brush stroke or a detail, but where the image is smeared away. At present, when in a situation where the other is a toxic, enemy rival, we beat our wings in search of a scapegoat, of which we find far too many. The reductive mechanism of the scapegoat, so ably described by Girard, can no longer function, since it requires a violent unanimity centered on a victim who is alleged to be guilty. Surrounded by enemies, the only recourse has been to pull back, extoll individualism, glorify the norms and decrees that protect my "rights"; we have litigated and adjudicated human relations to the extreme and withdrawn trust in all but a limited group. These cells of the social body are increasingly diverging from one another; they fragment society, the nation, into a jigsaw puzzle as Jérôme Fourquet suggests as *L'Archipel français*. Apropos, Solzhenitsyn warned us in his address at Harvard in 1978: "When all life is saturated with juridical relations, we have created an atmosphere of moral mediocracy that asphyxiates the best human impulses."

The pervasive litigiousness of human relations has another major inconvenience. Laws, rules, norms, prohibitions, etc., cannot foresee everything despite their efforts and complexity. As of the Middle Ages, a fable jested tellingly about this. A man had required that his wife draw up and sign a list detailing all her tasks. One day he fell into a river and pleaded with his wife to help him get out. After consulting the document, she replied, "That is not on my list!"

In the day-to-day experience of psychology and psychopathology, we understand why the detection and designation of the toxic other is so difficult and has posed for centuries such an arduous problem. It is because the other, the model, is unpredictable. It changes at any moment and alters interdividual relations. The other is at times a model, friend, partner, beloved and, over a seeming trifle, becomes an enemy rival, a detested adversary; or yet again springs up as an insurmountable obstacle in my path. The other is all these characters, alternatively, successively, sometimes simultaneously, and this makes his or her identification impossible, because no sooner detected and designated as a rival, does he or she become once again a kind, friendly model. Instantly we forget what that person was a minute ago.

These incessant variations of the other, these multiple metamorphoses, render it difficult, if not impossible, to characterize and therefore to identify. Mimetic psychotherapy aims at helping the patient face reality and recognize its mutability. If, in fact, the appearance of the other as rival transforms the interdividual relation into conflict, the rivalry can become a chronic condition. We have to learn how to see the masks of the model, the rival, and the obstacle in their fundamental unity and not freeze any particular role. We have to learn how to face up to reality, to see it for what it is, without reacting automatically.

Here is what Krishnamurti has to tell us: "By impartial observation, the door can perhaps open you up to yourself, and you come to know the dimension where there is no conflict and no time" (41). He confirms the intuitions that I am trying to spell out here: "I can only observe myself in term of my relations, because all life is relation" (26). Hindu wisdom resonates with mimetic psychology. This is why the thought of Eastern philosophers has known such success today. So many people are fans of the Dalai Lama, transcendental meditation, and like forms of mindfulness, of meditative consciousness-raising. Psychiatrists like the astute Christophe André have found this to be an extremely effective therapeutic process.

Why? Because Eastern philosophies, promoters of meditation, have the same goal as interdividual psychology: face up to reality before reacting "spontaneously" by unleashing the mimetic function of our brain, what I have called "the mimetic brain." As Krishnamurti enlightens us: "To see anything whatsoever with simplicity is one of the most difficult things to do. . . . Simplicity that allows us to look directly at something without fear, and at oneself, such as we are, without distortion; and if we lie, tell ourselves we lie, without dissembling or denial" (29).

This is what Krishnamurti calls impartial observation. To succeed in it, we must "free ourselves from familiar knowledge," meaning all our conditioning, all the mimetics of rivalry, all comparisons feeding resentment about everything we have been taught or forbidden. These millenary forms of wisdom are in tune with the most recent scientific discoveries. Our knowledge of mirror neurons teaches us that we are programmed to imitate, and therefore to compare, to desire what the other has or is—programmed therefore to fall into rivalry.

What can we do in this situation where our freedom is jeopardized in this way? The only opening to freedom that remains to us is the choice of the model. We must avoid any exclusive, demanding model, as this leads to fanaticism; instead, we need to choose a model or models who help us move forward, and we must never transform them into rivals or obstacles. In the modern world, this also involves the responsibility of the model, of the indispensable ones first of all, our parents. It is their responsibility to avoid conflict, to spell out what is forbidden without negotiating about it, and show the child that all their decisions are made for his or her welfare and interest. If we forbid them to touch fire, it is to prevent them getting burned. Explain, yes; justify oneself or negotiate, no. This principle of authority is conferred by the child on the parents because he or she trusts them. This trust must be worked on. The parents must make efforts to develop it through love, by a non-conflictual relation, and by constant encouragement, considering the needs of the child above all.

Responsibility accrues to all the models who succeed the parents: teachers, mentors, bosses, company executives, political leaders. All these models should display self-confidence in what they favor and what they forbid. Why? Because prohibition fortifies desire in the way that weightlifting relies on gravitational resistance to fortify muscles. The "self" of desire is structured by prohibition. If nothing is forbidden, nothing is desired. If nothing is desired, the "self" takes no shape, is not formed. This psychological reality is already revealed in Genesis. The tree is desired because it is forbidden. Prohibition is the only quality that distinguishes it from other trees. The desire for it constitutes a "self"; it introduces what is properly human and cast into the world upon the expulsion from an earthly paradise.

This is especially clear in the modern world where drugs proliferate. As of 1973, I have distinguished between the current phenomenon of drug addictions and their classic version, which was the preserve of few, as we find in texts about the Club des Hashishins by Théophile Gautier and Moreau de Tours. The current drug addictions spreading among us respond to a vital, deep-seated, essential need to experiment with desire in a desperate effort to construct a "self" for oneself, a "self" of desire. Permissiveness, the prohibition to prohibit, a generalized undifferentiation, leads young people to seek in drugs an ersatz of desire, which is experienced in and as the lack of something. They repeat the cycle incessantly: absorb the drug—sedation—lack. This lack is a caricature of desire, because it only seeks to disappear; it does nothing else but pursue its own sedation. As soon as the lack is appeased by another hit of the drug, the "self," which could have appeared or taken shape, is dissolved into nothingness. Desire, on the contrary, forges the "self," because it leads to action, to determined strategies to realize it. Little by little, this "self" in action goaded by desire builds itself up. If the desire is sustained, if the self succeeds in persisting in this effort by deferring the realization of its desire, this desire is transformed over time into will power.

X.

Scenarios of Alterity

For a long time, alterity has been at once dissimulated and revealed by various scenarios and representations. What these scenarios have in common is to show in all forms of alterity the aspect of rivalry, one that is sometimes abrupt and sometimes attenuated. Some examples will illustrate my point and confirm what I have been arguing for a long time: the clinical manifestation of mimetic desire is rivalry. A mise en scène of rivalrous alterity can play a cathartic role.

Rivalries Pacific or Violent

Gladiators, Bull Fights, Boxing Matches

Gladiators fight with lethal weapons. They know what awaits them when they enter the arena and present themselves before Caesar with the words: "Morituri te salutant" ("those who are about to die salute you"). The rivalry is nonetheless staged because the gladiators were not enemies. They fight without hatred, killing one another joylessly. These were comrades, colleagues, who knew the rules of the game and knew they could not elude them.

When the bull enters the arena, it could use the same words as the gladiators. Alterity is dissimulated here behind the guise of the brave matador fighting at the risk of his life against a furious monster. Here again, alterity is dressed up and represented as a death struggle devoid of hatred.

A boxing match stages a dangerous rival alterity in the guise of sport. The two adversaries are not enemies but often share a mutual antagonism and give battle mercilessly. The KO of one of them symbolizes the death of the "rival" other, but fortunately in most cases, he is still living. The kinship of these three scenarios of rival alterity concealed as sport is quite obvious.

Games of Chance and Games of Intelligence

Games of chance, lotteries, roulette, drawing straws in myriad situations, stage an alterity that is perennially feared and revered by humans: Destiny, Chance, Luck. Will the gods be with me or against me? The mask of the other is only revealed by the result: rival if I have lost; benevolent model and ally if I have won. The loser's only consolation is a possible rematch: tempt fate again, bet again and again against the luck that eludes me, this destiny which is playing with me. Consequently, addiction sets in, rivalry has become a chronic disorder, because the loser never gives up. There is no death here to end the combat. Gambling, the next deal of the cards, must always be resumed. If I have lost, I bet again to win this time. If I have won, I bet again to win more, because I see in this victory the proof that luck is with me and that destiny has finally decided to reward me.

As Dostoyevsky writes in *The Gambler*: "I won. I bet again and won again. . . . I should have stopped there, but a bizarre sensation took over me. I was defying fate, I wanted to snap my fingers at it, stick out my tongue. . . . I left the table stunned. I did not at all understand what had happened to me." Further on, he says: "I am always convinced that I should win. How does it happen that my stupid and shameful loss this morning did not shake that conviction?" This mythic rival—destiny, luck, divinity, chance—often represents the everyday rivalry of what Girard calls "the doubles," which designates mimetic rivals who derive their superiority and their happiness from the failure of the other, being imbued by feelings and emotions that accompany the fluctuations of the interdividual relation.

Games of intelligence like chess, poker, and bridge, stage a rival alterity where responsibility falls somewhat more, somewhat less, to the players. Chance and luck govern the deal of good or bad cards, but the player's skill matters a lot for the outcome of the contest. With the lottery, there are no good or bad players, whereas with card games and especially chess, the intelligence, skill, and strategy, of the player determine the outcome. Poker exhibits a droll resemblance to Marivaux's *The Game of Love and Chance*, about which Girard comments: "The lover is subject to the same randomness as the gambler."

This is where strategy and psychology come into play. Bluff in poker yields the expression "poker face," about which Girard notes: "One can shield oneself from chance by dissimulating one's desire." Gambling stages the alterity of everyday life: in love, competition, strategies of desire, politics, the essential role of dissimulation is worthy of Machiavelli.

Alcoholism

Two things strike me about alcoholism: Alcohol is considered by the heavy drinker as an alter ego, an other, at times a benevolent, consoling model, at times as an enslaving, dominating rival; furthermore, alcohol reveals the alterity of the "self." Alcohol is how Dr. Jekyll transforms into Mister Hyde. It reveals the consubstantiality of the model with the rival. The alcoholic cannot stand himself; his habitual "self" seems banal, uninteresting. Alcohol allows him to construct another "self," that of his rival desire and his resentment. When drunk, he can say anything; everything is permitted. Freed from every constraint, he is without moral or social inhibitions. It is against this ambition, this desire, that a conversation is necessary if you want to get him or her to give up drinking. These are the issues that have led the greatest experts on it to create Alcoholics Anonymous, with its twelve steps whose function is to exchange for this rival other, at once consoling and enslaving, another model, spiritual, divine, which alone can console and succor. Only an alcoholic who is "in remission" can help another alcoholic, because he or she represents a different model, an ally, who intervenes as an intermediary whose task is to walk ahead of the drinker and open the way to freedom. Obviously, there is something of an initiatory dimension

to this process, a vade mecum of metamorphosis, Mister Hyde becoming
again Dr. Jekyll.

Impersonators

Artists like Thierry Le Luron, Laurent Gerra, Veronic DiCaire, and still others make us laugh by imitating well-known figures. They demonstrate alterity by miming it: the orchestra begins, for example, *La mamma*, and here
Charles Aznavour comes onto the scene singing with the maw of Laurent
Gerra. One might say that Gerra imitates Aznavour; in primitive tribes, one
would say Aznavour has "possessed" Gerra (*The Puppet of Desire*, chapter 3).

In our culture, impersonation provokes admiration and laughter if the
performer voices a political figure speaking nonsense. In primitive societies,
the rituals involving possession is therapeutic for the possessed and beneficial
for the community. The representation of alterity, the fact that we see with
our own eyes that the "self" can be other, and that the other can become me,
is a striking recognition, always beneficial, of the alterity of my desire, of my
being, of my "self": the other being personated here is never a rival nor an
obstacle but still a model. This is why the impersonator's overt representations of alterity feel so good to us.

Impersonators, mimics, point us to the heart of mimetic psychology.
They perform two approaches that are the only route to freedom and well-
being, to wisdom: the choice of the model and the choice of the relation to
the model. The impersonator's choice always bears on a famous model that
Girard calls the "external mediator," someone known to us but distant from
us, beyond our reach. To imitate our next-door neighbor or our best friend
would not necessarily have good results; such a person would be an "internal
mediator."

The connection to this famous person is an interdividual relation that
is not conflictual, being a kind of homage to a star one admires, or a play-
ful imitation of a political figure; it is not rivalrous, never incurring revolt
or violence. The model remains a model, never a rival nor an obstacle; the
interdividual relation here is pacific. Another benefit of the scenic staging of
imitations is that the models are many, and one can switch from voices and
personalities at any time.

Terrorism

Here we find the counter example of a mimetism that spawns violence.

Terrorism is born of fanaticism, which is characterized by the choice of a unique model to the aggressive or violent exclusion of any and all others. The ascendancy of this unique model results in a mimetic submission to it, the inevitable desire to yield entirely to it, and to fiercely combat all the others. On the individual level, this psychological situation has been described by Pierre Janet as a secondary effect of hypnosis that he calls a "somnambulistic passion, born of the need to obey orders."

The engine of terrorism consists not only in the fanatical choice of a unique and indisputable model but also in the mimetic rivalry with other adepts of the same cause. There is a ghastly competition for horror: someone murders ten infidels in an act of self-sacrifice. I will kill still more in order to appear more deserving in the eyes of the model.

This is why I have explained for some time that drug addictions these days can only be countered by the emergence of a more attractive model, of a higher purpose, of collective ambition that is more motivating, and not at all by police suppression or psychiatric estrangement. For the same reason, I think that terrorism and Islamist fanaticism flourish amid the deliquescence of cultural and religious models in the West. Islamism is not the fault of Islam but our own.

Everyone needs a model, be it enforced from without or freely chosen. In *Valeurs actuelles* of July 4 and 10, 2019, Boualem Sansal states quite rightly: "With their apparel of feverish ascetics, their limitless cruelty, and their obsessional love of death, the Taliban and their regime have terrorized and fascinated thousands of young desperados around the world, but also drop-outs from the middle class. . . . They have been models to follow in Islamic culture. The imitation of the Prophet, of caliphs, of martyrs, guides, sheiks, chiefs, fathers, older brothers is an essential chapter of Islamic education. 'You have in the Messenger of Allah an excellent model for whoever hopes in Allah and in the Last Day and who invokes Allah frequently' (Qur'an 33:21)."

It is not simply a matter of detoxifying the drug addict or of deradicalizing the fanatics, which comes down to criticizing and discrediting their models. That is an empty, useless undertaking. Rather it is a matter of reconstructing our Western cultural model; of making it attractive, powerful, tempting; making it capable of drawing to it those who are somewhere else in their head. It is not by excusing ourselves and relativizing our culture, our values, our actions, our ambitions, that we will lead others to rejoin us. There is a need here for a vast program at the political level involving the refoundation of values that is beyond the scope of this book.

Alterity without Rivalry: Masks

I have just gone over some scenarios of rivalrous alterity in what is often their pacific and ludic manifestations, but at times their violent and lethal ones, as in the last example. But it is equally possible to represent alterity as such, without rivalry, owing to the use of masks.

A masquerade allows for being an other in the eyes of everyone and dissimulating the "self" behind this other. The other so "created" is capable of doing what the "self" could not do: evil in the case of the arch criminal Fantômas, good in the case of Zorro, for example. What we learn from Zorro is an other who can perform exploits that the "self" cannot. Behind the mask and the garb of Zorro, Don Diego de la Vega, an idle guitar-strumming young man, becomes the redoubtable and invincible righter of wrongs. In one of the episodes, Don Diego hosts a ravishing young aristocrat and serenades her with his guitar. She finds him enjoyable but frivolous, too "soft." One day, she is carried off by some bandits, and Zorro comes to the rescue. The next day, she declares to Don Diego: "Now there's a real man!" She has fallen in love with him without seeing his real face. Don Diego confides to his valet: "Can one be jealous of oneself?" The "self," I've argued, is the product of desire. This desire is mapped onto a model. It is, in sum, the desire of the other that produces the "self": hypnosis generates in the subject an other, who is another "self" of the other desire, a new "self" with its own attributes, its own consciousness, memory, speech, and emotions. By taking on a mask, the "self" produces another "self," the "self" of an idealized desire. This new "self" can perform extraordinary exploits that the original "self" cannot. The model of this new "self" is the ideal "self," a phantasy of the "everyday self."

This new identification with an ideal "self" is formidably adept, as Zorro has just shown us.

The mask can also be a virtual other behind which one can hide and which is capable of doing what one can no longer do oneself. Thus, Romain Gary, suffering from a kind of fatigue and disillusionment, thinks that he can no longer write and publish *Au-delà de cette limite, votre ticket n'est plus valable*. Before long, he creates an "alter," another self, but new, and the "alter" wins the Prix Goncourt! The book's title expresses the resourceful victory of alterity: *La vie devant soi*, written by Emile Ajar, the other created out of whole cloth as a mask for Romain Gary.

In *Le Figaro* of March 20, 2020, Jacques Julliard quotes Cicero's remark in *Pro Murena*: "I have not tried to put on a mask," and Julliard reminds us that the Roman orator is speaking of persona, which in Latin means a theatrical mask. What Cicero meant, we are told, is: "I refuse to perform a role, I present myself as you see me." Theater actors of antiquity wore masks, which made them others whose roles they played. The mask was called "persona." The actor only becomes the character as masked: you had to otherize yourself to become someone onstage. Today, social networks are swarming with masks and pseudo-identities that allow people to dissimulate themselves to spread "fake news," to malign or calumniate. A negative virtual world is being created, in which numerous adolescents lose themselves. Their chances of facing up to reality are diminished accordingly.

XI

The Otherizing of the Gods

The gods themselves only present themselves as masked, assuming the features of another, whose familiar and harmless bearing would not frighten people. Jupiter, the king of the gods, is often attracted by the beauty of a young woman, a Phoenician princess for example, and we find him otherized, metamorphosed, into a cute, gentle white bull grouped with the royal herd. Europa cannot fail to notice this superb animal. She approaches, caresses it. The bull makes eyes at her and calmly rubs up against her. It lowers its legs down toward her. Charmed by this, Europa jumps on its back. In a vigorous bound, the bull takes her off and flies through the air, far away to a new land, which shall be called Europa, where he is free to make love to her. On another occasion, Jupiter is smitten by Leda, who lies dreaming beneath a tree, and the god transforms—otherizes—himself into a magnificent swan that attracts Leda, who throws it a piece of bread. The swan stretches its neck and climbs onto the bank. Leda caresses it, takes it in her arms, and the trick works. And yet again, Jupiter is seduced by the beauty of the young Danae; in one version of the myth, Jupiter notes that this woman is fond of silver. So the god is transformed into a shower of gold coins raining down from the sky.

Stupefied, Danae hastens to collect the coins and hide them in her bed, where Jupiter's desire is gratified.

In the *Odyssey*, Athena is ever coming to the aid of her protégé Ulysses, appearing to him in various features so as not to be recognized by him. We could easily multiply such examples.

In the Bible, which I am considering here as host to mythological stories without reference to religious belief, Yahweh never shows himself, but he intervenes throughout the text. It is what theologians call theophanies. God orders Abraham to sacrifice his son; then at the last minute, Abraham is ordered to replace his son at the altar with a ram. God speaks, he commands, but does not show himself. He acts and intervenes spectacularly in getting Moses to lead his people out of Egypt and goes so far as to divide the Red Sea for them to pass through it, and then closes it again around Pharoah's army. God appears to Moses in the form of a burning bush, which is not incinerated and gives him the ten commandments. The first of these affirms that it is he, Yahweh, who commands him to lead his people out of slavery and give them freedom.

Still, without taking a religious position or staking out ground for belief or faith, it is clear that God, in the Gospels, is incarnated, otherizes himself, takes human form to appear to men and women and to deliver his message, show them the way of Truth and Life. God is an embryo, then a fetus in the womb of the Virgin Mary. He is born just like any human and grows up. From the baby in the crèche, we have the child Jesus. He leads his life in secrecy, then reveals himself in his last three years. The story is well known, but I am struck by two things:

- Jesus represents an alter ideal, an other that every human can take as a model and lead his and her life in his light. According to the text, he is God the Father in the form of Jesus, the Son, who presents to humans the ideal Alterity, at once like them and radically different from them.
- On the cross, Jesus says a few words and I find these particularly striking: "Eloi, Eloi, lama sabachthani," "My God, my God, why have you forsaken me?" This God, who throughout biblical narratives has spoken to his prophets, to his people, who has directly intervened to save or punish them—this God does not answer his son, does not answer humans. In this silence, I have a sense of the end of history.

God will never again speak to humans. He has said everything there is
to tell them! It is up to them from now on to understand, to choose,
to conduct themselves. I will risk the thought that Jesus is the Other,
the mask, the character that God takes on to live among humans
and deliver his message without terrorizing nor coercing them. God
otherizes himself in order to appear to humans and propose a model
without imposing it. By the words of Jesus and by his action and
conduct, God has told humans everything that he could; he has shown
humans everything he could show. Jesus himself says: "If you have seen
me, you have seen the Father."

Jesus, then, is the absolute model, the one we are to follow and not imitate. To imitate him would develop with regard to him a mimetic desire and
would entail a dose of mimetic rivalry that is inadmissible and incompatible
with the path that has been laid out. To follow Christ, on the contrary, as
he invites each one of his disciples to do, is to acknowledge that he comes
before me, precedes me. Recognizing this desire as anterior to mine shelters
me from any rivalry. Clearly, between God and his Other, between God
and his mask made present as his son, to speak in human terms, there is an
exceptional interdividual relation, a union of thought, of love, of confidence,
so absolute that the essence, the nature of this relation is hypostasized as
the Holy Spirit. This way of seeing the mystery of the Trinity could perhaps
reconcile Christians with the other monotheisms that do not allow for the
idea of God in three persons. The otherizing of God in a form that is "pre-
sentable" to humans in order to speak to them directly and at length, and to
live among them, in order to hold before their eyes a living model—all this is
made explicit in John's Gospel where we read at the outset: "The Word was
God," and "the Word was made flesh," and furthermore "The Word came in
among his own." If we read these utterances back to back, it is clear that God
has otherized himself, has been transformed as human in order to be able to
"come in among his own."

Conclusion

There is a unity to living things, to nature, to life, and to worlds. Since 1981, I have striven to establish the fact that the physical world is governed by Newtonian physics, universal gravitation, which accounts for the attraction and repulsion of bodies in space. A first effort to discover a principle of the same kind in psychology was that of Franz Anton Mesmer, who postulated the existence of a universal magnetic fluid. In accounting for attraction and repulsion, he spoke of "forward intention and pulling back" of humans among themselves. At the time, I proposed that the world of humans is governed by a unique principle of the same kind, universal mimesis, which is imitation in space, repetition in time, and even reproduction in the species. I have since understood that Newtonian physics should be completed by Einsteinian relativity and then by quantum physics, and that the latter could interfere with realities of the psyche, particularly in the memory of space and time. In psychology, every day, at every instant, it is a matter of recognizing reality, of accepting the alterity that pervades us, of gradually relativizing our desires with the help of numerous models of all kinds. These are sometimes the least expected, as they lead us on an initiatory path toward permanent transformation by accepting to die to our desires of yesterday, to our "self" of yesterday, and thus to move forward toward *wisdom*. But in practice? In daily life, we have to adapt to reality, once having recognized it. So, in the light of all of this, what recommendations are available?

- Choose the model. This is the only path to freedom that remains to us, because the desire of the model will spawn our own, which will create our "self," with the understanding that certain models are imposed on us: parents first of all, and thereafter the cultural models that preside as we grow up.
- Consolidate this freedom by choosing several models, by constructing a patchwork of models, each of which exhibits a personality, an attitude, an ambition, a lively potential. We have to see clearly that the same person may represent for the patient two different models and so the choice is complicated.

A man of distinction, CEO of his company, comes to me for a consultation; he has anxiety attacks that occur unexpectedly, unrelated to any particular event. Psychotherapy leads him to reveal that he loves his wife, but that he is also in love with another woman, whose main attraction consists in her being a foreigner living abroad, which allows him to be discriminating, to avoid, in his terms, "mixing up brushes on the palette." On the lookout for his model, I ask him to talk about his father, whom he describes as a loving parent during his childhood and youth, as the dad who shared his life with mom. But later, he discovers that his father had a secret liaison, another wife, another household. That is where the problem arises and the anxiety: which of the two models to choose from? The loving father of the family or the lover indulging in an intense passion on the side. The choice is frightful, because he finds himself between two aspects of the same person. Which one is to be his model: return to his wife and consolidate his family relations, or travel more and more often to rejoin the other woman, the idealized love of his life? The choice is difficult and obviously causes anxiety, even anguish. The psychotherapist's role consists in clarifying the choice, in helping him see the two aspects of his model and to accept that duality, without resentment or rejection. The aim is to get him to face up to reality, to help him in this decision; to do so he might choose another model, perhaps a mentor or a psychotherapist, without being forced to choose between loving his dad or despising the adulterous father.

- Understand clearly what is meant by a model in daily experience—one that is friendly, sympathetic, helpful—and what is meant by a rival, who is aggressive, critical, disagreeable. Accept the fact that in daily life the geometry of this relation is variable and that we must not take too seriously and fasten on the model relation nor on the rivalrous one. When the rival kicks in, never forget that he or she was a positive model and could become one again at any time. When the model appears to be all kindness, never forget that he or she was a rival and could return to this role at any moment. When I say "not take seriously," I mean do not get carried away with the model, do not divinize it, nor get carried away in the other direction and demonize the rival.
- Avoid adopting a unique, all-powerful model, which leads to fanaticism and utter estrangement.
- Do not at all cost allow any of the chosen models to transform into a rival. If this transformation occurs, give up on both the model and the rival; avoid them. Don't fight them; avoid conflict at all costs.
- Accept the fact that the model can be a rival intermittently, and that the model and the rival can show up several times a day. Learn to welcome the model who crops up and to manage the situation when it becomes a rival in order to favor its return to the role of model.
- If we divinize the model, the danger is that he or she will abuse the dominant position. We know that power corrupts and that absolute power corrupts absolutely. Consequently, the divinized model will enslave us; we become his or her pet. Thus Valmont writes to Madame de Merteuil in *Dangerous Liaisons*: "Your orders are charming, the way you give them is still more amiable. You could make one cherish despotism. . . . I regret that I am no longer your slave."

If, on the contrary, we demonize the rival, we will live in a permanent state of stress: *fight or flight*? Flight is best, but it is not always possible for many reasons: financial, familial, religious, economic, etc. And *fight*? The conflict can

become violent with regrettable consequences: nervous breakdown, shout-
ing, blows, even the death of one the protagonists. *Fight* can also become a
chronic condition and result in a kind of cold war, as we see in the relation
between the characters played by Jean Gabin and Simone Signoret in the
film *Le Chat.*

In the end, one of the parties of *fight* can lose and surrender and become
the household pet of the other. There can be no doubt that if one does not
wish to become the puppet of desire, the plaything of mimetic mechanisms,
it is necessary to learn how to face up to and recognize reality; to see clearly
the mimetic mechanisms at work; and to identify the incessant gambits of
mimetic desire as it leads to the transformation, the metamorphosis of the
model from confederate ally and friend into sinister, jealous, inimical rival.
It is necessary to have a clear view of mimetic rivalry in human relations and
accept it. To get there, one needs to learn early on to see what's going on,
become interested in people, in psychology, and learn to respond to it, to
adjust one's behavior, to adapt oneself to the other in every situation. To get
there, one needs an initiation to what I call "psychopolitics" (*Psychopolitics*,
2012), a politics that is enlightened by mimetic psychology, which is always
in service to reality, as regrettable as it may turn out; one needs to never "take
one's desires for realities," which is to project one's ideology onto the real
and wish to force reality to conform to one's illusions. To paraphrase Kant,
a politics without mimetic psychology is blind, but a psychology without
political savvy is powerless.

- Wisdom consists in the management of alterity. The first step consists
  in seeing the alterity, and the second in accepting it in its different
  aspects, in adapting to it in its transformations and metamorphoses.
  Ultimately, wisdom will arrive at a condition of plasticity, allowing us
  to change our personality depending on the alterity one is dealing with.
  Michel Leiris reports on his encounter with an Ethiopian sage, Malkam
  Ayyahu, who could change his "self" at the whim of his encounters and
  relations with others, by drawing upon what he called a "cloakroom of
  personalities."
- There is, finally, another requirement that bears on the responsibility
  of the model: that of the natural ones, parents, first of all; and that
  of inevitable models thereafter, such as teachers, bosses, superiors,

political figures, etc. Here the choice is at once the most difficult and dangerous. Because the choice of the model comes down to the problem of freedom, which these days is jeopardized by advertising, the press, and especially social networks. The free choice of the model ultimately implicates the responsibility of each and every one: the choice of Ben Laden or Nelson Mandela is not neutral; it implies a heavy responsibility for the one who makes it, even if one is influenced by pressures exercised in the media. There is, therefore, in the choice of the model, a heavy responsibility on the part of the one who chooses it as well as on the part of the model who solicits imitation.

• In choosing a spouse, a companion, an associate, a partner, it does not suffice to ask if we admire or esteem him or her enough to adopt him or her as a model; wisdom consists in adopting as the model the *relation* that one has observed with couples, for example, who function well together in a lasting union that one admires for that fact. In choosing a partner, one needs to analyze the relation that is established with him or her, and not the physical and mental qualities or flaws of the other such as they are.

References

Aretaeus of Cappadocia. *Of the Causes and Signs of Acute and Chronic Disease.* In *The Extant Works of Aretaeus, the Cappadocian.* Edited and translated by Francis Adams. 1856. Reprint, Boston: Milford House, 1972. Available as *De causis et signis acutorum morborum (lib. 2)* at Perseus Digital Library, Tufts University. http://www.perseus.tufts.edu/hopper/collections.

Aristotle. *Poetics.* Translated by Stephen Halliwell. Cambridge, MA: Harvard University Press/Loeb Classical Library, 1995.

Ferry, Luc. *Qu'est-ce que la vie réussie?.* Paris: Grasset, 2002.

Fourquet, Jérôme. *L'Archipel français.* Paris: Le Seuil, 2019.

De Funès, Julia. *Développement (im)personnel.* Paris: Editions de l'Observatoire, 2019.

Gautier, Théophile. "Club des Haschischins." *Revue des Deux Mondes* (Paris), February 1, 1846.

Girard, René. *Things Hidden since the Foundation of the World: Research Undertaken in Collaboration with Jean-Michel Oughourlian and Guy Lefort.* Translated by Stephen Bann and Michael Metteer. Stanford, CA: Stanford University Press, 1987.

———. *Resurrection from the Underground: Feodor Dostoevsky.* Translated by James G. Williams. East Lansing: Michigan State University Press, 2012.

———. *Resurrection from the Underground: Feodor Dostoevsky.* East Lansing: Michigan State University Press, 2012.

Khayat, David. *Enquête vérité: Vous n'aurez plus jamais peur du cancer*. Paris: Albin Michel, 2018.

Kojève, Alexandre. *Introduction to the Reading of Hegel: Lectures on the Phenomenology of Spirit*. Translated by James J. Nichols Jr. Ithaca, NY: Cornell University Press, 1980.

Krishnamurti, Jiddu. *Se libérer du connu*. Paris: Stock, 1970.

Leiris, Michel. *La Possession et ses aspects théâtraux chez les Ethiopiens de Gondar*, précédé de *La Croyance aux génés zâr en Ethiopie du Nord*. Paris: Fata Morgana, 1989.

Luccesi, Jacques. *Le Désir d'être un autre: Essai de psychologie sociale*. Paris: Harmattan, 2018.

Oughourlian, Jean-Michel. *The Puppet of Desire: The Psychology of Hysteria, Possession, and Hypnosis*. Translated by Eugene Webb. Stanford, CA: Stanford University Press, 1991.

———. *Le Désir: Énergie et finalité*. Paris: Harmattan, 1999.

———. *The Genesis of Desire*. Translated by Eugene Webb. East Lansing: Michigan State University Press, 2010.

———. *Psychopolitics*. Translated by Trevor Cribben Merrill. East Lansing: Michigan State University Press, 2012.

———. *The Mimetic Brain*. Translated by Trevor Cribbed Merrill. East Lansing: Michigan State University Press, 2016.

———. *Cet autre qui m'obsède*. Paris: Albin Michel, 2017.

Oughourlian, Jean-Michel and Jacques-Marie Coldefy. *Approche psychosomatique de la pratique médicale et chirurgicale*. Paris: Privat, 1975.

Pigeaud, Jackie. *La Maladie de l'âme*. Paris: Les Belles Lettres, 2006.

Plato. *The Complete Dialogues*. Edited by Edith Hamilton and Huntington Cairns. New York: Pantheon/Bollingen, 1964.

Staune, Jean. *Notre expérience a-t-elle un sens? Une enquête scientifique et philosophique*. Paris: Presse de la Renaissance, 2007.

Research Bibliography

Anspach, Mark Rogin. *A charge de revanche: Les formes élémentaires de la réciprocité*. Paris: Le Seuil, 2002.

———. *Œdipe mimétique*. Paris: Le Herne, 2010. [*Oedipus Unbound: Selected Writings on Rivalry and Desire*. Edited by Mark R. Anspach. Stanford, CA: Stanford University Press, 2004.]

Bandera, Cesàreo. *Mimésis conflictiva*. Madrid: Gredos, 1975.

———. *The Sacred Game: The Role of the Sacred in the Genesis of Modern Literary Fiction*. University Park: Pennsylvania University Press, 1994.

Bateson, Gregory. *La Cérémonie du Naven*. Paris: Minuit, 1986. [*Naven: A Survey of the Problems Suggested by a Composite Picture of the Culture of a New Guinea Tribe Drawn from Three Points of View*. Stanford, CA: Stanford University Press, 1965.]

———. *Vers une écologie de l'esprit*. 2 vols. Paris: Le Seuil, 1977, 1980.

———. *Steps to an Ecology of Mind*. New York: Ballantine, 1972.

———. *Une unité sacré*. Paris: Le Seuil, 1996. [*A Sacred Unity: Further Steps to an Ecology of Mind*. New York: Hampton Press, 2005.]

Bernheim, Henri. *Hypnotisme et suggestion*. Paris: Doin, 1910.

Bertagna, Louis, and Monique Vigny. *Dépression et couple: Un entretien avec Louis Bertagna*. Paris: Ardix mèdical, 1995.

Blackmore, Susan. *La Théorie des mèmes: Pourquoi nous nous imitons les uns les autres*. Paris: Max Milo, 2006.

Brague, Rémi. *Europe: La voie romaine*. Paris: Gallimard, 1992. [*Eccentric Culture: A Theory of Western Civilization*. Translated by Samuel Lester. South Bend, IN: St. Augustine's Press, 2002.]

Carroll, Lewis. *Alice au pays des merveilles*. Translated by Jacques Papy. Paris: Gallimard, 1994.

Canetti, Elias. *Masse et puissance*. Paris: Gallimard, 1986. [*Crowds and Power*. Translated by Carol Stuart. New York: Farrar, Straus, and Giroux, 1984.]

Choderlos de Laclos, Pierre. *Œuvres complètes*. Paris: Gallimard, 1979.

Clément, Olivier. "Dionysos et le réssuscité." In *Evangile et révolution*. Paris: Centurion, 1968.

Clérambault, Gaëton de. *L'Automatisme mental*. Paris: Les Empêcheurs de penser en rond, 1992.

———. *L'Erotomanie*. Paris: Les Empêcheurs de penser en rond, 2002.

Corneille, Pierre. *Le Cid*. Paris: Pocket, 2005.

Corraze, Jacques. *De l'hystérie aux pathominies*. Paris: Dunot, 1976.

———. *Les Communications non-verbales*. Paris: Presses Universitaires de France, 1992.

Crébillon fils. *Le Sopha*. Paris: Flammarion, 1995.

Cyrulnik, Boris. *Un merveilleux malheur*. Paris: Odile Jacob, 1999.

Cyrulnik, Boris, Patrice van Eersel, Theirry Janssen, Christophe André, Jean-Michel Oughourlian, and Pierre Bustany. *Votre cerveau n'a pas fini de vous étonner*. Paris: Albin Michel, 2012.

Damasio, Antonio. *L'Autre moi-même: Les nouvelles cartes du cerveau, de la conscience et des émotions*. Paris: Odile Jacob, 2010. [*Self Comes to Mind: Constructing the Conscious Brain*. New York: Pantheon, 2010.]

———. *L'Erreur de Descartes*. Paris: Odile Jacob, 1995. [*Descartes' Error: Emotion, Reason, and the Human Brain*. New York: Putnam, 1994; revised Penguin, 2005.]

———. *Le sentiment même de soi: Corps, émotions, conscience*. Paris: Odile Jacob, 2003. [*The Feeling of What Happens: Body and Emotion in the Making of Consciousness*. New York: Harcourt, 1999.]

———. *Spinoza avait raison: Joie et tristesse, le cerveau des émotions*. Paris: Odile Jacob, 2003. [*Looking for Spinoza: Joy, Sorrow, and the Feeling Brain*. New York: Harcourt, 2003.]

Dawson, David. *Flesh Becomes Word: A Lexicography of the Scapegoat, or the History of an Idea*. East Lansing,: Michigan State University Press, 2013.

Delay, Jean. *Les Dissolutions de la mémoire*. Paris: Presses Universitaires de France, 1947.

Deniker, Pierre. *La Dépression: Fin du tunnel.* Paris: Doin, 1998.

Derrida, Jacques. *La Dissémination.* Paris: Le Seuil, 1972. [*Dissemination.* Translated by Barbara Johnson. Chicago: University of Chicago Press, 1981.]

Descartes, René. *Méditations métaphysiques.* Paris: Flammarion, 2011. [*Meditations on First Philosophy.* Translated by J. Cottingham. Cambridge: Cambridge University Press, 1996.]

Dewhurst, K. *Thomas Willis as a Physician.* Los Angeles: University of California Press, 1964.

Dostoyevsky, Feodor. *Crime et châtiment.* Translated by André Markowicz. Paris: Actes Sud, 1996. [Multiple translations are available.]

———. "L'Eternel mari." In *L'Adolescent,* translated by Boris de Schloezer. Paris: Gallimard, 1956. [*The Eternal Husband and Other Stories.* Translated by Richard Pevear and Larissa Voloknonsky. New York: Random House, 1997.]

Dumouchel, Paul. *Le Sacrifice inutile: Essai sur la violence politique.* Paris: Flammarion, 2011. [*The Barren Sacrifice: An Essay on Political Violence.* Translated by Mary Baker. East Lansing: Michigan State University Press, 2015.]

Dupuy, Jean-Pierre. *Le Sacrifice et l'envie.* Paris: Calmann-Lévy, 1992.

Duroy, Lionel. *Le Chagrin.* Paris: J'ai lu, 2010.

Eliade, Mircea. *Rites and Symbols of Initiation.* New York: Harper, 1965.

———. *Traité de l'histoire des religions.* Paris: Payot, 1970.

Erickson, Milton. *Altération par l'hypnose des processus sensoriels, perceptifs et psychophysiologiques.* New York: Irvington, 1980.

———. "L'hypnose et son induction." In *Experimental Hypnosis,* edited by Leslie M. LeCron, [pp. 70–114]. New York: Macmillan, 1952.

Ey, Henri. *Manuel de psychiatrie.* Paris: Masson, 1967.

Falret, Jean-Pierre. *Observations sur le projet de loi relative aux aliénés.* Paris: Adolphe Everat, 1837.

Faure, Henri. *Hallucinations et réalité perceptive.* Paris: Presses Universitaires de France, 1969.

———. *Les Appartenances du délirant.* Paris: Presses Universitaires de France, 1966.

Freedberg, David, and Vittorio Gallese. "Motion, Emotion, and Empathy in Esthetic Experience." *Trends in Cognitive Science* 11, no. 5 (2007): 197–203.

Freud, Sigmund. *Au-delà du principe de plaisir.* Paris Payot, 2010. [*Beyond the Pleasure Principle.* Translated by James Strachey. New York: Liveright, 1967.]

———. *Psychologie des foules and analyse du moi.* Paris: Payot, 2012. [*Group Psychology and the Analysis of the Ego.* Translated by James Strachey. New York: Liveright, 1960.]

————. *Psychologies de la vie amoureuse*. Translated by Olivier Mannoni. Paris: Payot, 2012. [*Sexuality and the Psychology of Love*. Translated by James Strachey. New York: Macmillan, 1963.]

Gallese, Vittorio. "Embodied Simulation from Neurons to Phenomenal Experience." *Phenomenology and the Cognitive Sciences* 4 (2005): [23–48].

————. "Intentional Attunement: A Neurophysiological Perspective on Social Cognition and Disruption." *Brain Research* 1079 (2006): [15–24].

————. "The Manifold of Interpersonal Relations: The Quest for a Common Mechanism." *Philosophical Transactions of the Royal Society of London B* 358 (2003): [517–528].

————. "The Shared Manifold Hypothesis: From Neurons to Empathy. *Journal of Consciousness Studies* 8 (2001): [33–50].

————. "Two Sides of Mimesis: Girard's Mimetic Theory, Embodied Simulation, and Social Identification." *Journal of Consciousness Studies* 16, no. 4 (2009): [21–44].

Gans, Eric. *The Scenic Imagination: Originary Thinking from Hobbes to the Present Day*. Stanford, CA: Stanford University Press, 2008.

Garrels, Scott. "Imitation, Mirror Neurons, and Mimetic Desire." *Contagion: Journal of Violence, Mimesis, and Culture* 12–13 (2006): [47–86].

————, ed. *Mimesis and Science: Empirical research on Imitation and the Mimetic Theory of Culture and Religion*. East Lansing: Michigan State University Press, 2011.

Girard, René. *Achever Clausewitz*, interviews with Benoît Chantre. Paris: Carnets Nord, 2007. [*Battling to the End*. Translated by Mary Baker. East Lansing: Michigan State University Press, 2010.]

————. Afterword to *Le Péché originel à la lumière de la Résurrection: Bienheureuse faute d'Adam* by James Alison. Translated by François Rosso. Paris: Editions du Cerf, 2009. [*The Joy of Being Wrong: Original Sin through Easter Eyes*. New York: Crossroad/ Herder & Herder 1998.]

————. *Des Choses cachées depuis la fondation du monde*, with Guy Lefort and Jean-Michel Oughourlian. Paris: Grasset, 1978; Livre de Poche, 1983. [*Things Hidden since the Foundation of the World: Research Undertaken in Collaboration with Jean-Michel Oughourlian and G. Lefort*. Translated by Stephen Bann and Michael Metteer. Stanford, CA: Stanford University Press, 1987.]

————. *La Conversion de l'art*. Texts collected by Benoît Chantre and Trevor Cribben Merrill. Paris: Flammarion, 2010.

————. *La Violence et le sacré*. Paris: Grasset, 1972; Le Livre de Poche, 1998. [*Violence and the Sacred*. Translated by Patrick Gregory. Baltimore: Johns Hopkins University Press, 1977.]

————. *Les Feux de l'envie: William Shakespeare*. Translated by Bernard Vincent. Paris: Grasset, 1990. [*A Theatre of Envy: William Shakespeare*. New York: Oxford University Press, 1992.]

————. *Les Origines de la culture*. Paris: Hachette, 2006. [*Evolution and Conversion: Dialogues on the Origins of Culture*. London: Continuum, 2008.]

————. *Mensonge romantique et vérité romanesque*. Paris: Grasset, 1961; Hachette Pluriel, 1999. [*Deceit, Desire and the Novel: Self and Other in Literary Structure*. Translated by Yvonne Freccero. Baltimore: Johns Hopkins University Press, 1996.]

Goleman, Daniel. *L'intelligence émotionnelle*. Translated by Thierry Piélat. Paris: J'ai lu, 2003. [*Emotional Intelligence: Why It Can Matter More Than IQ*. New York: Bantam, 1995.]

————. *Cultiver l'intelligence émotionnelle*. Translated by Thierry Piélat. Paris: Robert Laffont, 2009. [*Working with Emotional Intelligence*. New York, Bantam, 1998.]

Guillaume, Paul. *L'Imitation chez l'enfant*. Paris: Alcan, 1926; Presses Universitaires de France, 1969.

Hart, Sybil, and M. Legerste, eds. *Handbook of Jealousy: Theory, Research, and Multidisciplinary Approaches*. New York: Wiley-Blackwell, 2010.

Hirigoyen, Marie-France. *Abus de faiblesse et autres manipulations*. Paris: Lattès, 2012.

Janet, Pierre. *Névroses et idées fixes*. 2 vols. Paris: Alcan, 1898.

Joyce, James. *Gens de Dublin*. Paris: Pocket, 2003. [*Dubliners*. New York: Penguin, 1993.]

Kafka. *Le Procès*. Translated by Claude David and Alexandre Vialette. Paris: Gallimard, 1987. [*The Trial*. Translated by Breon Mitchell. New York: Schocken, 1999.]

Keukelaere, Simon de. "Des Découvertes révolutionnaires en sciences cognitives: Les Paradoxes et dangers de l'imitation." *Automates intelligents* 63 (2005).

————. "La Violence humaine, imitation ou mèmes: Critique d'un point de vue girardien." *Automates intelligents* (2002).

Lacan, Jacques. *De la psychose paranoïaque dans ses rapports avec la personnalité*. In *Premiers écrits sur la paranoïa*. Paris: Le Seuil, 1975.

————. *Ecrits*. Paris: Le Seuil, 1966. [*Écrits: The First Complete Edition in English*. Translated by Bruce Fink. New York: Norton, 2006.]

La Planche, J., and J.-B. Pontalis. *Vocabulaire de la psychanalyse*. Paris: Presses Universitaires de France, 1967.

Le Bon, Gustave. *Psychologie des foules*. 1895. Paris: Presses Universitaires de France, 1963. [*The Crowd: A Study of the Popular Mind*. Zurich: ETH Zurich. https://www.files. ethz.ch/isn/125518/1414_LeBon.pdf.]

Le Doux, Joseph. *Le Cerveau des émotions*. Paris: Odile Jacob, 2005.

Leiris, Michel. *La Possession et ses aspects théâtraux chez les Ethiopiens de Gondar, précédé de La Croyance aux génés zâr en Ethiopie du Nord*. Paris: Fata Morgana, 1989.

Le Rider, Jacques. "Nietezsche et Baudelaire." *Littérature* 86 (1992): [85–101].

Malony, Clarence, ed. *The Evil Eye*. New York: Columbia University Press, 1976.

McDonald, Brian. "Violence and the Lamb Slain: An Interview with René Girard." *Touchstone Magazine*, December 2003.

Meltzoff, Andrew, and Jean Decety. "Elements of De Developmental Theory of Imitation." *The Imitative Mind: Developments, Evolution, and Brain Bases*, [19–41]. Cambridge: Cambridge University Press, 2002.

———. "Out of the Mouths of Babes: Imitation, Gaze, and Intentions in Infant Research; The 'Like Me' Framework." *Mimesis and Science: Empirical research on Imitation and the Mimetic Theory of Culture and Religion*. Edited by Scott Garrels. East Lansing: Michigan State University Press, 2011.

———. "What Imitation Tells Us about Social Cognition: A Rapprochement between Developmental Psychology and Cognitive Neuroscience." *Philosophical Transactions of the Royal Society of London: Biologic Sciences* 358 (2003).

Meltzoff, Andrew, Jean Decety, and Alison Gopnik. *Words, Thoughts, and Theories*. Cambridge, MA: MIT Press, 1997.

Meltzoff, Andrew, Jean Decety, and M. K. Moore. "Imitation of Facial and Manual Gestures by Human Neonates." *Science* 198 (1977): [75–78].

Merrill, Trevor Cribben. *The Book of Imitation and Desire: Reading Milan Kundera with René Girard*. New York: Bloomsbury, 2013.

———. "The Labyrinth of Values: Triangular Desire in Milan Kundera's Dr. Havel after Twenty Years." *Heliopolis: Culture Civilitá Politica* 8, no. 1 (2010): [69–75].

Mesmer, Franz Anton. *Le Magnétisme animal*. Paris: Payot, 1971.

———. *Mémoire sur la découverte du magnétisme animal*. 1779. Paris: Allia, 2006.

Molière, Jean-Poquelin. *Le Misanthrope*, 1666. [Multiple English translations are available.]

Murat, Laure. *L'homme qui se prenait pour Napoléon: Pour une histoire politique de la folie*. Paris: Gallimard, 2011.

Muray, Philippe. *Exorcismes spirituels*. Vol. 2, *Les Moulins de Panurge*. Paris: Belles Lettres, 1998.

Musil, Robert. *L'homme sans qualités*. Translated by Philippe Jaccottet. Paris: Le Seuil, 2011. [*Man without Qualities*. Translated by Sophie Wilkins. New York: Knopf, 1996.]

Nietzsche, Friedrich. *L'Antéchrist*. Paris: Union Générale d'éditions, 1974. [*The Antichrist*. In *The Portable Nietzsche*. Translated by Walter Kaufmann. New York: Viking Press, 1968 [565–656].

———. *Lettres Choisies*. Edited by Marc de Launay. Paris: Gallimard, 2008.

———. "Nietzsche à la lettre." Nietzsche à la lettre. nietzschealalettre.pagesperso-orange.fr.

———. *Oeuvres philosophiques complètes*. Vols. 1 and 8. Paris: Gallimard, 1974–1977.

———. *Selected Letters of Nietzsche*. Edited by Christopher Middleton. Chicago: University of Chicago Press, 1969.

Nygren. Anders. *Eros et Agape*. 3 vols. Paris: Aubier, 1958.

Ramachandran, Vilayanur. *A Brief Tour of Human Consciousness*. Paris: Pi, 2005.

————. "The Neurology of Self-Awareness." *Edge Magazine* 8 (2007). http://www.edge.
org/3rd_culture/ramachandran07/ramachandran07_index.html.

Proust, Marcel. *A la recherche du temps perdu*. 3 vols. Paris: Gallimard, 1954. [*Remembrance
of Things Past*. Translated by C. K. Scott Montcrieff. New York: Random House,
1932.]

Ricoeur, Paul. *Philosophie de la volonté*. Vol. 2, *Finitude et culpabilité*. Paris: Aubier,
1960–1988.

Rifkin, Jeremy, and K. Beeching. *Une Nouvelle conscience pour un monde en crise*. Paris: Actes
Sud, 2012.

Rizzolattti, Giacomo. "I Know What You Are Doing: A Neurophysiological Study." *Neuron*
32 (2001).

Rizzolatti, Giacomo, and Michael Arbib. "Language with Our Grasp." *Trends in
Neurosciences* 21 (1998): [188–194].

Rizzolattti, Giacomo, and Laila Craighero. "The Mirror Neuron System." *Annual Review of
Neurosciences* 27 (2004).

Rizzolattti, Giacomo, Leonardo Fogassi, and Vittorio Gallese. "Les neurones miroirs." *Pour
la science* 351 (Jan. 2007).

————. "Neurophysiological Mechanisms Underlying the Understanding and Imitation of
Action." *Neuroscience Review* 2 (2001): [661–670].

Rizzolattti, Giacomo, and Corrado Si–nigaglia. *Les Neurones miroirs*. Translated by
Marilène Raiola. Paris: Odile Jacob, 2008.

Robert, Marthe. *La Révolution psychanalytique*. Paris: Payot, 1964.

Rougemont, Denis de. *L'Amour et l'occident*. Paris: Flammarion: 2005. [*Love in the Western
World*. Translated by Montgomery Belgion. Princeton, NJ: Princeton University Press,
1983.]

Rousseau, Jean-Jacques. *Discours sur l'origine de l'inégalité parmi les hommes*. Paris: Livre de
Poche, 2005. [Multiple translations in English are available.]

————. *Lettre à d'Alembert sur les spectacles*. Paris: Flammarion, 2003.

————. *Rêveries du promeneur solitaire*. Paris: Livre de Poche, 1978. [Multiple translations
in English are available.]

Roustang, François. *Influence*. Paris: Minuit, 1991.

————. *Le Bal masqué de Giacomo Casanova*. Paris: Minuit, 1985.

————. *Un Destin si funeste*. Paris: Minuit, 1977.

Roustang, François, and Pierre Babin. *Le Thérapeute et son patient*. Paris: L'Aube, 2000.

Scheler, Max. *Nature et formes de la sympathie*. Paris: Payot, 2003. [*The Nature of Sympathy*. Translated by Peter Heath. New Haven: Yale University Press, 1954.]

Selye, Hans. *The Stress of Life*. New York: McGraw-Hill, 1956.

Sérieux, Paul, and Joseph Capgras. *Les Folies raisonnantes: Le Délire d'interprétation*. Paris: Alcan, 1909.

Serres, Michel. *La Guerre mondiale*. Paris: Le Pommier, 2008.

———. *La Traduction*. Paris: Minuit, 1974.

———. *Le Malpropre: Polluer pour s'approprier?* Paris: Le Pommier, 2008.

———. *Rome: Le Livre des fondations*. Paris Grasset, 1983.

Sicard, Marie Claude. *Danse avec les renards*. Paris: Editions du Palio, 2007.

Sloterdijk, Peter. *Colère et Temps*. Translated by Olivier Mannoni. Paris: Maren Sell, 2007.

Sow, I. *Psychiatrie dynamique africaine*. Paris: Payot, 1977.

Spinoza, Baruch. *L'Ethique*. Traanslated by Mibert Misrahi. Paris: Éditions de l'Eclat, 2005.

Stekel, Wilhelm. *La Femme frigide*. Paris: Gallimard, 1948.

Tarde, Gabriel. *Les Lois de l'imitation*. Paris: Alcan, 1895. [*The Laws of Imitation*. Translated by Elsie Clews Parsons. New York: Holt, 1903.]

Tolle, Eckhart. *The Power of Now: A Guide to Spiritual Enlightenment*. Vancouver, BC: Namaste, 1977.

Trevarthen, Colwyn, Theono Kokkinaki, and Geraldo Fiamenghi. "What Infants' Imitations Communicate: With Mothers, with Fathers, with Peers." In *Imitation in Infancy*, edited by J. Nadel and G. Butterworth. Cambridge: Cambridge University Press, 1999.

Vega, Lope de. *Le Chien du jardinier*. Translated by Frédéric Serralta. Paris: Gallimard, 2011.

Voltaire. *Candide ou l'Optimisme*, 1759. [Multiple translations in English are available.]

Watzlavick, Paul, Janet Beavin, and Don Jackson. *Pragmatics of Human Communication*. New York: Norton, 1967.

Zweig, Stefan. *Conscience contre violence*. Bègles, France: Le Castor astral, 2004.

Index

Printed and bound by CPI Group (UK) Ltd, Croydon, CR0 4YY

09/06/2025

14685842-0002